TAKE-OFF

American All-Girl Bands During WWII

TONYA BOLDEN

Alfred A. Knopf
New York

For my editor, Erin Clarke, who, to borrow from George Bernard Shaw, dreams things that never were and says, Why not?

THIS IS A BORZOI BOOK PUBLISHED BY ALFRED A. KNOPF

Text copyright © 2007 by Tonya Bolden

Jacket photographs courtesy of Culver Pictures; Special Collections/Archives, John B. Coleman Library, Prairie View A&M University; *DownBeat* magazine.

Published in the United States by Alfred A. Knopf, an imprint of Random House Children's Books, a division of Random House, Inc., New York.

KNOPF, BORZOI BOOKS, and the colophon are registered trademarks of Random House, Inc.

www.randomhouse.com/teens

Educators and librarians, for a variety of teaching tools, visit us at www.randomhouse.com/teachers

Library of Congress Cataloging-in-Publication Data
Bolden, Tonya.
Take-off : American all-girl bands during WWII / by Tonya Bolden. — 1st ed.
   p. cm.
Includes bibliographical references and index
ISBN 978-0-375-82797-6 (trade) — ISBN 978-0-375-92797-3 (lib. bdg.)
1. Women jazz musicians—United States—Juvenile literature. 2. Big bands—History—1939–1945—Juvenile literature. [1. Women jazz musicians. 2. Big bands.] I. Title.
ML3929.B65 2007
784.4'81650820973—dc22
2006024523

BOOK AND CD MANUFACTURED IN CHINA

May 2007

10 9 8 7 6 5 4 3 2 1

First Edition

CONTENTS

Intro   3

Part 1
"The Band Was on Fire":
ADA LEONARD'S ALL-AMERICAN GIRL ORCHESTRA   10

Part 2
"We Played All the Way up to New York!":
THE PRAIRIE VIEW STATE COLLEGE CO-EDS   26

Part 3
"What Are We Gonna Do for a Drummer?":
THE INTERNATIONAL SWEETHEARTS OF RHYTHM   37

Outro   54

Glossary   62

Notes   64

Selected Sources   70

Recommended Reading   72

Recommended Listening   72

Illustration and Text Credits   73

Acknowledgments   74

Index   75

WHAT IS Swing?

Harry James

"This is indeed the $64 question of popular music," bopped Bill Treadwell in the opener of his 1946 not-so-big *Big Book of Swing*. "Finding a hen's tooth . . . or rolling a peanut up Pike's Peak with your nose—these are all child's play compared to getting a definition of the most debated word in jazz that will make everybody happy." When Treadwell sampled re-bops from top talents, the following were in the mix—

Cootie Williams: "Define it? I'd rather tackle Einstein's theory!"

Benny Goodman: "Free speech in music."

Tommy Dorsey: "Jazz was modern music in its infancy and Swing is the infant grown up with all the vigor of eight to the bar come of age."

Harry James: "Swing is improvised music, arranged and played in the various styles of big time bands."

Johnny Desmond: "Swing is a combination of simple melodic lines written against a rhythmical background and played in many variations of a single theme."

Ella Fitzgerald: "Jazz or Swing—it's all the same as long as it has that beat."

W. C. Handy: "Swing is the latest term for ragtime, jazz and blues. You white folks just have a new word for our old-fashioned hot music."

Ella Fitzgerald

> ## GIRL MUSICIANS.
> ## Brass, rhythm, saxes. Young, attractive, modern readers. Steady engagements. AIRMAIL photo, details. "Take-off"?

This was the start of a June 1941 help-wanted ad for the Swinghearts. An outfit like that clashed with the dominant idea of what was respectable for female bands. Many people thought it downright devilish for a woman to make a sax wail, produce walking-bass plucks, let loose hot licks on skins, or make other moves in service of the most dynamic dance music of the day. Some

"If I were seeking an effect of power, of heavy beats . . . I should certainly not go to work with a group of girls," Phil Spitalny told Etude *magazine in 1938, four years after he launched the band that became the Hour of Charm. Its name came from the Sunday-night radio show, which premiered in 1935. Many Americans deemed this super-successful orchestra, with its mostly mellow music, the ideal all-woman band.*

called this jazz "jump," others "jive." In the end, "swing" thrived.

Swing gave wings to the jitterbug and other ecstatic, acrobatic dances. Swing gave rise to a slew of slang—from A ("Apple" for Harlem) to Z ("zooty" for flashy or extreme—as in the zoot suit).

In between, you had "canary" (gal singer), "cat" (guy in a swing band), "hep" (progenitor of "hip"), and "take-off": to solo, improvising to your soul's delight.

Swing's biggest boosters—the "big bands." These twelve-to-twenty-piece (or larger) orchestras bounced out

Jitterbugs, June 1938. A few years later, a Life *magazine article about how a mass of teens let loose at a Harry James concert in the Big Apple had the headline "Jitterbugs Jam James's Jive Jag." Some fans cut the rug in the aisles. Others jittered in their seats.*

of the Big Apple and the Big Easy; they clocked out of K.C., Chi-Town, and Cincy.

A big band's rhythm section usually had an 88 (piano), doghouse (bass violin), and drum set—ride cymbal a must! Its brass section, a triplet of trumpets and a pair of trombones (aka tram—aka slushpumps, sliphorns, and sackbutts). The reed section might have one of each from the family of sax (soprano, alto, tenor, baritone)—and a licorice stick (clarinet), perhaps. Fiddles (violins), belly-fiddles (guitars), a woodpile (xylophone), and a grunt horn (tuba) were also in the swing of things in some big bands.

Big band leaders were piano players—take Count Basie for one—singers, with Cab Calloway a prime example, and hide-beaters like Gene Krupa. These cats and scores of other legends fronted bands that served up tunes that still make folks jump, jive, and wail today. "One O'Clock Jump," "Stompin' at the Savoy," and "In the Mood" are just a few. On the list, too, the song some say gave swing the big kickoff: the 1932 Duke Ellington hit "It Don't Mean a Thing (If It Ain't Got That Swing)."

Some big bands featured a canary or had a "fem" on the 88's. As for the rest of the band—lassies, step back! That was the rule.

"Good jazz is hard, masculine music with a whip to it." So said music maven Marvin Freedman in an early 1941 issue of Chicago-based *DownBeat,* the era's primo

Cab Calloway is most remembered for the song "Minnie the Moocher," with the scat "Hi-De-Hi-De-Hi-De-Ho." Cab once led a band with his older sister, Blanche, also a singer. In the 1930s, she broke bad with her own all-guy band: Blanche Calloway and Her Joy Boys. Blanche also had an all-girl band for a beat.

Cover boy, 1945. Gene Krupa was certainly among the flashiest, if not truly the "world's fastest," drummer as billed.

Detroit's Graystone was one of the hottest spots for top "orks," as hepcats called orchestras. Like many places, the Graystone didn't allow racially mixed audiences. Monday was its "colored night." This poster was for a Monday night in 1933.

● ● ● ● ● ● ● ● ● ● ● ● ● ● ● ●

Page one of an August 8, 1938, Life *magazine feature. Seven months earlier, Benny Goodman's ork headlined the mega-successful first swing music concert at New York City's famed Carnegie Hall. As historian Gerald Early explains, "whites dominated the scene" when* Life *ran this article putting its stamp of approval on a style of music that "fifteen years earlier most mainstream publications considered degenerate." So it's not surprising that the article jumps off celebrating white bandleaders: slushpumper Tommy Dorsey, who led a band with his older brother Jimmy (reeds) until the two fell out; singer Bob Crosby (younger brother of capital crooner Bing); vibes-ster Red Norvo; and clarinetists Artie (not "Arty," as spelled in the caption) Shaw and Benny Goodman, the "King of Swing." Page two spotlights "Swing's Black Royalty": Duke Ellington, Count Basie, King Oliver, and Louie Armstrong, aka "Satchmo."*

jazz magazine ("the *Beat*" to hepsters). Like many guys, Freedman didn't think gals could truly dig swing or any other jazz. "Women like violins, and jazz deals with drums and trumpets." Many women winced at this dig— *"Gimme a break!"* The Swinghearts was one band that blasted Freedman's bum rap. And this chick band was by no means the first.

Pioneering female jazz bands include Marian Pankey's Female Orchestra (all black) and Babe Egan's Hollywood Redheads (all white). Ina Ray Hutton and Her Melodears, hatched in 1934, was one of the first swinging all-girl bands to really take-off.

Six months after that ad for the Swinghearts, a chain reaction sparked by an American tragedy—Pearl Harbor—ushered in a shift in the fortunes of more fem cats.

● ● ●

During World War II, roughly 16 million American men served in the armed forces abroad and on bases stateside.

Ina Ray Hutton and Her Melodears, 1937. Ina was a tap-dance kid turned showgirl. Her band had some truly fine musicians, but she—aka the "Blonde Bombshell of Swing"—was not one of them. Ina sang okay. The only other instrument she played was her body. "In some places, policemen had to surround the stage as Hutton danced and gyrated to the music," wrote Sally Placksin in her book American Women in Jazz. *"Wild Party" was one of the platters Ina's ork cut. The band appeared in feature films and starred in movie shorts. Its first such mini-musical was* Feminine Rhythm *(1935); the last,* Swing, Hutton, Swing *(1937). Ina swung away from her Melodears to front an all-guy band in 1939.*

Some band, somewhere, June 11, 1942. One of many all-girl bands of the 1940s whose history is a mystery.

With the war's depletion of manpower for home-front work, women were urged to stand in the gap. At a time when few middle-class women worked outside the home, the Office of War Information (OWI) produced piles of propaganda hailing women at *hard, masculine* work a hallmark of patriotism.

Many Janes and Jills got the hang of suiting up in overalls and work boots. Ruthies and Rosies learned to make aircraft for Boeing and lay track for the B&O Railroad. Maes and Marys became "milkmen."

What was a woman with a beat to do—a woman who'd rather riff than rivet? With scads of cats drafted and volunteering for military service, more chicks jumped at the chance to bandstand.

They were young—some of them still teenagers.

Most were down with getting dolled up to make the grade as "attractive."

Some were "modern readers"—that is, able to play jazz charts; others couldn't read music but could play like nobody's business.

"Take-off?"

Oh, yeah.

This OWI poster signaled that a woman working in a munitions plant, and, by extension, gals doing other "men's work," was as heroic as a woman serving with the American Red Cross and armed forces, from a WAAC (Women's Army Auxiliary Corps) to a WAVE (Women Accepted for Volunteer Emergency Service in the Navy). Women in the Coast Guard were SPARS (from the Coast Guard's motto, Semper Paratus, *"Always Ready"). Flygirls were WASPs (Women Airforce Service Pilots). The Marine Corps' women's division was simply called the Women's Reserve. (In 1943, the Women's Army Auxiliary Corps became the Women's Army Corps, so WAACs became WACs.)*

Part 1

"The Band Was on Fire"
ADA LEONARD'S ALL-AMERICAN GIRL ORCHESTRA

Lawton, Oklahoma–born Ada Leonard, 1937. Her father was an actor. Her mother's talents included costume designing and music making (several instruments). Ada was doing a song-and-dance act at age three. About fifteen years later, she made her debut in burlesque at the 1933–1934 World's Fair, held in Chicago, her home base. Ada went on to make a name for herself as a classy stripper. She also snagged bit parts in a few flicks. One is the 1937 comedy Stage Door, *about a bunch of young women hungry to make it in showbiz. The cast included several silver-screen legends: Lucille Ball, Katharine Hepburn, and Ginger Rogers among them.*

Ada Leonard's All-American Girl Orchestra was among the few bands working on the night of December 7, 1941. Most entertainment joints were closed. Much of America was in lights-out mode and on the listen-out for air-raid sirens. Fear of another attack was especially intense on the West Coast. But Ada's band wasn't playing there or for civilians, but for troops at Fort Belvoir, outside D.C.

When the band reached the fort, the security check lasted one, two—*five* hours, remembered trumpeter Janie Sager. "We waited and waited and waited, and the [bus driver] had to turn the motor off because you couldn't waste gas. We were freezing. . . . By eleven o'clock at night they finally got themselves organized enough to realize that we weren't enemies. We were the USO show."

The show went on.

"I don't know what in the heck time we got through that night." Nor did Janie recall what-all the band played. Whatever the tunes, chances are she wowed the crowd if she took off.

Born in Milwaukee and raised in Green Bay, Janie's journey began with study of the violin. She won a spot playing classical music on a local radio show at age ten. Shortly after that triumph, tragedy struck. While riding her brand-new bike, Janie was hit by car. Its back wheel wrecked her left hand. *Hasta la vista,* violin.

Janie later found another outlet for her music jones, psyched by the sight of a girl working a cornet with one hand at a high school concert. Janie got herself a horn lickety-split. It was a lousy horn, but she worked it—"I could play 'Come to Jesus' and make it swing." Soon this girl was swinging with local dance bands.

Janie switched back to serious study of the violin at the all-women Stephens College in Columbia, Missouri (class of '34). But the horn had a lock on her soul. She kicked it to Chicago, where she studied trumpet formally with Edward Llewellyn, the Chicago Symphony Orchestra's principal trumpet player in the early 1930s. She also worked her chops on the fly, at jam sessions with a mix of bands—black, white, all-guy, all-gal. Janie jammed *pro* with several bands, too. One was Rita Rio and Her Mistresses of Rhythm (Rita's theme song: "La Cucaracha").

After Rio's band, Janie Sager played with the Chicago Women's Symph. On the side, she blew with bands that played bar mitzvahs and other private socials. When she heard about the great getting up of a new chick band—Janie fell in.

During the band's days in the woodshed—rehearsing, rehearsing, *rehearsing*—agent Al Borde was braining on bookings. He insisted on a bandleader with popularity and pizzazz. His top pick—Ada Leonard. Janie and

Rita Rio had several orks. She quit the band biz in 1940 with hopes of becoming a movie star.

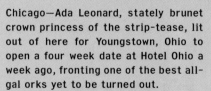 **from the *Beat:* June 15, 1941**

Chicago—Ada Leonard, stately brunet crown princess of the strip-tease, lit out of here for Youngstown, Ohio to open a four week date at Hotel Ohio a week ago, fronting one of the best all-gal orks yet to be turned out.

The band, a 16-piecer which actually has been together for about a year and a half, was formerly headed by saxist Bernice Little. . . . Some of the best fem cats in the trade compose the outfit, chicks who have been with Spitalny, Rita Rio, Ina Ray Hutton, the Coquettes, and so on.

• • • • • • • • • • • • • •

This article was headlined "Strip-Tease Ada Leonard Fronts Ace Fem Outfit."

Ada in the spotlight with her band. The musicians include Janie Sager (middle row, fourth from left), sax player Bernice Little (to Janie's left), and drummer Dez Thompson, an Hour of Charm alumna (top row, far right).

her bandmates got pretty salty—*"Oh, please—a striptease?"*

When Al approached Ada, she was doing her number at the Rialto, outside Chicago in Joliet, and she was past ready for a change of pace. She had recently been in the stage musical *A Night at the Moulin Rouge.* So had Rita Rio's band. As Ada eyed Rita, she thought, *I can do that.*

Janie Sager ended up cutting Ada some slack, even became her coach. The ex-stripper proved a quick study in the art of batoning a band.

● ● ●

Many new bands debut in dives, but Ada's started out at a

swanky place, at Chicago's State-Lake Theater, and in a prime slot: Christmas week, 1940. It wasn't long before Ada's band got noticed. And even though Ada didn't engage in wild-party gyrations like Ina Ray Hutton, in venue after venue, she had to put up with catcalls—"Take it off!"— versus shouts for one of her musicians to take-off.

It was after a string of well-received performances that the USO tapped Ada's band for camp shows. The gals had been on the camp-show circuit for a while by December 7, 1941. They stayed on that circuit for many more weeks: two shows a night, six days a week—sometimes seven, if drafted to do a hospital show on their day off.

With the USO, Ada's musicians made about eighty bucks a week. Back then, the minimum wage was thirty cents an hour, and a loaf of bread cost about a dime. Ada and her gals typically had more expenses than male musickers, from makeup to wardrobe. For civilian audiences, Ada's band usually wore a sweet blouse-and-long-skirt combo. When performing for troops, their skirts were blue, their blouses red-and-white-striped.

Based on conversations with Janie Sager, Sherrie Tucker, author of *Swing Shift: "All-Girl" Bands of the 1940s*, reconstructed a typical USO show of 1942. Taking it from the top, Ada's band played "an instrumental piece like 'Bugle Call Rag,' " a jumper with riffs on the military wake-up call, "Reveille."

After an instrumental, a chick chirped: "Perhaps tenor

A USO lounge in Chicago's Union Station, February 1943. The coalition of charities making up the USO (United Service Organizations) formed in 1940. Sponsoring camp shows was just one way the USO fulfilled its mission to care for members of the military. It also created places where GI Joes, jarheads, flyboys, and swabbies could play cards, throw darts, watch flicks, dance to tunes flowing from a jukebox or radio, or simply write letters that began "Dear Mom," "Dear Dad," or "Dear Darling."

Happy campers at an unidentified USO camp show, April 1943.

from the *Beat:* February 1, 1942

Why not let the girls play in the big name bands? In these times of national emergency, many of the star instrumentalists of the big name bands are being drafted. . . .

[T]here are some girl musicians who are as much the masters of their instruments as are male musicians. They can improvise; their solos are well-defined and thought-provoking and show unlimited imagination.

● ● ● ● ● ● ● ● ● ● ● ● ● ● ● ● ●

This article by drummer Viola Smith was headlined "Give Girl Musicians a Break!—Idea." Viola praised reedman Woody Herman for giving trumpeter Billie Rogers a spot in his band. Viola's article sparked quite a battle of words among the *Beat*'s readers. Their salvos were printed in its letters-to-the-editor column, "Chords and Discords."

saxophonist Brownie Slade would do one of her vocal numbers, stirring up the crowd's emotions with a ballad popular during the war—'White Cliffs of Dover' or 'Once in a While.' "

"White Cliffs of Dover" rhapsodizes about England's breathtaking white lime cliffs facing the English Channel, once the nation's nature-made defense against invaders from continental Europe. "White Cliffs" longs for "joy and laughter / and peace ever after"—a better tomorrow "when the world is free." (The other song, "Once in a While," pines for a lost love.)

Following such a ballad, dancer Mary Sawyer took center stage. She may have done a bit of ballet or tap, or a snatch of cancan. Next up—Janie Sager, "regaling the troops with her renowned rendition" of "Concerto for Trumpet" by Harry James.

Janie also took requests. "What's your favorite song?" she called out, then played the winning pick with piano and bass backup. After Janie came a comedy routine: some slapstick or stand-up, perhaps. Somewhere along the way, Ada aced a cooey love song, aka a "torch song," like "I Don't Want to Set the World on Fire (I Just Want to Start a Flame in Your Heart)." Coming full circle, Ada's band wrapped with an instrumental.

When Ada Leonard's ork wasn't on the USO campshow circuit, they were plenty busy playing ballrooms, theaters, and clubs. Tracking the band's dates is possible because, as Sherrie Tucker explains, "the group was now considered important enough to list in *DownBeat*'s 'Where the Bands Are Playing' column."

The band also rated updates in the *Beat.* One such item in a spring 1942 issue noted that the All-American Girl ork had been "playing army camps up and down the West Coast." It had shared the stage with Jackie Cooper (a star in the *Our Gang* movie shorts as a kid) and the fright-wig wearing, harp-playing Harpo Marx.

As for Ada's band's book, beauty was in the ear of the listener. Some jazz fiends found its repertoire more sweet than swing. In a bit on the band in a December 1942 issue of the *Beat,* Bob Fossum quoted Ada as saying: "Girl bands should not play too much jazz," and "People don't expect girls to play high-powered swing all night long. It looks out of place." The writer had checked the band at a one-nighter in Janesville, Wisconsin, at the Armory (where the legendary National Guard battalion known as the Janesville 99 had spent their training days). Fossum felt the band definitely lived up to Ada's expectations. He said it "concentrated on pops and standards. The little gut-music the girls did play was limited to stock arrangements of 'One O'Clock,' 'St. Louis Blues,' etc." The show was not without some sizzle: "Drummer Dez Thompson stole the show with her rock-bound beat and flashy solos."

In time, Ada's band offered up more swing. A critic

Viola Smith, aka the "female Gene Krupa," came out of Mount Calvary, Wisconsin. She had her first gigs as a kid with her seven sisters (the Schmitz Sisters) in the early 1920s. In the late 1930s, with sister Mildred, she started the Coquettes, fronted by singer Frances Carroll. When "Give Girl Musicians a Break!" appeared, Viola was waiting for her union card for Local 802, the New York City–area chapter of the American Federation of Musicians (AFM). In spring 1942, she joined Phil Spitalny's Hour of Charm, based in the Big Apple.

who caught the ork in the Big Apple in late summer 1943 declared it "definitely on the jump side." Months later, another critic who checked it out in Columbus, Ohio, said, "When the band went through a jivey arrangement of 'Seven Nights in a Bastille,' they put up a strong argument against those who claim only male musicians can handle fast music."

"The band was on fire," remembered drummer Florence Liebman, "Fagel" to family and friends. She joined Ada's ork in 1944, the year tenor sax player—and take-off titan—Ethel Kirkpatrick was brought on board.

Fagel deemed the band's repertoire "unbelievable. It was a man's book." For chicks with a beat, their own measure of success was how well they played like a top cat. "The first thing they'd say to you is, play like so-and-so, play like Coleman Hawkins," remembered Janie Sager. She spent a lot of years playing like Bunny Berigan and Roy "Little Jazz" Eldridge. Time spent emulating was time not spent cooking her own style.

• • •

As for Fagel Liebman, as a kid, she had a habit of hitting out rhythms on tabletops and whatnot around her home in Brooklyn, New York. As a teen, she bought a drum set with twenty-five bucks she saved up, and she ended up in an all-girl quartet booked for summers at Jewish resorts.

Everything young Fagel knew about the drums she taught herself by ear.

Ada Leonard
AND HER
ALL-AMERICAN   GIRL ORCHESTRA

FEATURING
MARTHA STUART
DEZ THOMPSON   MARIAN GANGE
FRANCES SHIRLEY   RITA KELLY
THELMA KAY   MARY COMBATTELLI

Currently
2nd Successful
U.S.O. Tour

THE ALL-STAR
GIRL DANCE BAND
OF 1943

Thanks
To All Our Loyal
Fans—Coast to Coast

Personal Manager GEORGE LIBERACE
Exclusive Management FREDERICK BROS. MUSIC CORP.
NEW YORK   •   CHICAGO   •   HOLLYWOOD

This ad for Ada's ork shows that the band was clearly going up! Frederick Brothers didn't handle peewees. The new booker and the personal manager no doubt had a hand in the band's picking up the pace. George Liberace was the older brother of Wladziu Valentino Liberace—"Lee" to family and friends, and simply "Liberace" on stage—the classically trained pianist who gained fame for playing pop and for his bedazzling costumes and flamboyant ways.

Listening.

Listening.

Listening.

She listened to big bands on the radio. She listened to records on her family's wind-up phonograph. She listened so much that she got to know "everyone's licks."

Fagel forever cherished chances to see the best bands live, from Ellington's at the Apollo Theatre in uptown Manhattan to Goodman's at the Paramount down in Times Square. "And when I saw Gene Krupa, something just happened to my insides. I was never the same after that."

Fagel looked back on her days with Ada's band as "the first really thrilling musical time of my life because that was all jazz." Before that, she had played with an Hour of Charm–type band led by Al D'Artega (and featured in the 1944 film *You Can't Ration Love*). Fagel gave the maestro his due as a "great arranger," but he "didn't feel jazz at all," she lamented. "I only left because I wanted to play more jazz," added Fagel, who still could not read music.

When Ada Leonard's band started really feeling jazz, its threads changed. "As the band's *sound* swung harder, with jazzier arrangements, more up-tempo numbers, and more improvised solos, its *look* became softer, as if to ensure the band's overall reception as acceptably feminine," explains Sherrie Tucker.

So out went the sweet blouse-and-long-skirt outfits. In came frilly, flouncy gowns, some of them strapless. For sisters swinging a sax—*ouch!* Strapless gowns meant neck straps digging into their skin.

Trumpeter Norma Carson remembered one of the group's getups as "these strange-lookin' pink dresses with ruffles down the front all the way to the floor." Ironing those dresses "was murder. On a suitcase—that's the way you do it on the road."

Ironing ruffles on a suitcase wasn't the only drag. Sometimes a public bathroom, say, in a train station, was

During the war, a range of commodities—food to fuel—was rationed.

Ouch!

Ada's band wasn't the only all-girl ork to suit up really femme. Some hide-beaters actually played in high heels. One writer tells of brass- and reed-playing fem cats being told to paint their lips with Mercurochrome instead of lipstick, which would smudge and wear off. In some bands, eyeglasses were a no-no. A chick had to either invest in contact lenses (not as easy on the eyes as the ones today) or memorize all the music and pretend to be reading charts when on stage. When this photo of Joan Lee's "lively" ork appeared in the *Beat* (June 15, 1943), dateline Talmage, Pennsylvania, the band was "kept busy with nite clubs, single dance engagements and radio work." No word as to whether Joan put something around her shoulders before she started swinging her sax.

their dressing room. Meals were often catch-as-catch-can. Janie Sager never forgot the standard fare when traveling by train out west for the USO—"those darn Fred Harvey sandwiches were the thinnest little piece of ham you ever saw in your life. You could see through it. And that rotten white bread. And they'd clamp it together, and that was a sandwich." (During WWII, the Fred Harvey Company had a lock on food concession for troop trains on the Santa Fe Railway. Decades earlier, its founder had established a chain of restaurants servicing railway stations in the West, with the fare served up by the fabled waitstaff, the Harvey Girls.)

Lame though the Fred Harvey sandwiches were, Janie

Jane Olive Sager, circa 1946. Janie left Ada's ork in late 1942 and settled in L.A., where she hooked a job at a defense plant. But then came a band spot—"Boy, did I dump that [job] in a hurry." The band was Johnny Richards's (once) all-male band. Janie's other gigs in the 1940s included a day job with a CBS radio band, the Victory Belles. Its leader was Peggy Gilbert (reeds, vibes, vocals), who fronted several all-girl bands from the 1920s to the 1940s.

admitted that sometimes they were "like a turkey dinner." Besides, she knew that lousy sandwiches were the least of many people's problems.

Legions of Japanese, Italians, Germans, and other "persons of enemy nationality" suffered suspicion of disloyalty and were forced to relocate. More than 120,000 people spent some or all of the war in internment camps in California, Colorado, and Texas, among other states, with very few guilty of treason or espionage.

Black Americans constantly contended with discrimination in almost every arena. "Strange fruit," a metaphor for lynch victims, about which jazz singer Billie Holiday first sang in 1939, could still be seen, especially in the South: "Southern trees bear strange fruit, / Blood on the leaves and blood at the root."

And then there was the warfare. Thousands of civilians lost loved ones. Thousands of soldiers came home with minds messed up and body parts gone.

Janie Sager was forever haunted by a special request when Ada's band was doing a hospital show. A GI, once a trumpeter himself, asked that Janie come to his bedside and play a Bunny Berigan solo (from "I Can't Get Started"). "And he was a stump," she told Sherrie Tucker fifty years later. "He had no arms, no legs, just this face, and he stared at me, and I'll never forget those eyes. . . . They were the most terrifying eyes yet, at the same time, so pitiful. And I had to look at those eyes, and you know, you can't blow a horn when you laugh or cry. But somehow I just said, 'Dear God, I've got to do this for this guy.' "

Eating "darn" Fred Harvey sandwiches, ironing on a suitcase, and a neck strap bite hardly qualify as the height of hardship, and on the plus side, the chicks in Ada Leonard's All-American Girl Orchestra were doing what they chose to do—what they *loved* to do. As they did their thing, they helped fellow Americans bounce out of the wartime blues for a moment in time.

"Music builds morale," said FDR, as President Franklin Delano Roosevelt was known. He wrote these words in an April 1943 thank-you letter to the secretary of the National and Inter-American Music Week. Music, the president added, "inspires our fighting men on battlegrounds abroad and in training camps at home. It spurs soldiers on the production front to new goals. It refreshes all of us, young and old alike, as we move forward in our wartime tasks to inevitable victory."

America abounded in "Victory!" talk and with V-for-Victory products, from pins, buttons, and brooches to photo frames. There were war bonds to buy "For Victory." There were Victory Gardens and Victory Films. There was V-mail: correspondence to troops written on special letter sheets, which were miniaturized by microfilm stateside, then enlarged overseas for distribution to soldiers.

In 1943, Uncle Sam began recruiting entertainers to make V-discs, records not to be retailed but booted free of

Singer, dancer, actress, bandleader, and "Queen of the Trumpet" Valaida Snow in a 1935 production of the musical revue Blackbirds *(tunes by Eubie Blake) at London's Coliseum Theatre (now the London Coliseum). By then, this Chattanooga chick had showcased her talents elsewhere in Europe, the Far East, the Middle East, and Russia. Valaida was cutting swing platters in Copenhagen when Nazis nabbed her. (Denmark had been under German occupation since spring 1940, and Hitler hated jazz and all things black.)*

charge to the men and women "Over There," risking their lives for Victory!

Some men, military and civilian, had the cockamamie idea that it was an all-girl band's patriotic duty to go on post-show dates. Like other women's bands, Ada's had to deal with guys they didn't dig bugging them, heavy-hitting on them,

from *Band Leaders:* November 1944

In this article, Joy Cayler speaks of heartthrobs and heartbreak: her high school sweetheart so disapproved of her horn playing and her hope to go pro that he dumped her. A few years later, she met a serviceman who was "more than proud of my abilities and ambitions."

trying to grope them, and worse. The gals almost always maintained a buddy system to guard against mashers as they dealt with other rigors of the road. (During later USO tours, the food situation got better.)

"I would have to say there were times when we were so tired that we literally thought we were gonna die," Fagel Liebman remembered. "Once on a train we were so tired— we hadn't laid our bodies down on a bed in I don't know how long—that we put newspapers on the floor and lay on the floor of the train. And we would dream of baths and showers. And, of course, a week in a theater or something was like heaven. One-nighters, it was very rough. But if you wanted to play, that's what you had to do at that time. For me, there was never any question, ever. If it came with the package, then I bought the package. I had to play to breathe and that was it."

The B-side of a V-disc. "Chickery Chick" is about a chicken fed up with just giving out a plain ole "chick-chick," and so one day takes off with a shout-out that starts "CHICKERY CHICK, cha-la-cha-la / check-a-la romey" and ends "Can't you see CHICKERY CHICK is me?" Until late 1944, the only records some union musicians made were V-discs. In the summer of 1942, AFM president James Caesar Petrillo had called for a halt on the waxing of new commercial sides in his battle with record companies for musicians to get royalties for music played on the radio and on jukeboxes.

Part 2

"We Played All the Way up to New York!"
THE PRAIRIE VIEW STATE COLLEGE CO-EDS

Clora Bryant was ripping to make whatever move she needed to make to keep playing her trumpet—"I said, 'If there's this girl band there and I can play my horn, then that's where I was going to go!'"

"There" was Prairie View College in southeast Texas, not far from Houston. The year: 1943.

Sixteen-year-old Clora was a senior at Terrell High in the north Texas town of Denison, near the Oklahoma border. Clora was one of three children her father raised solo after Mrs. Bryant died when Clora was two.

Brass section of the Prairie View Co-Eds.

The administrative building of Prairie View (now Prairie View A&M University), circa 1940. The school began as the Alta Vista Agricultural and Mechanical College of Texas for Colored Youths in 1876. It was created by an act of the Texas legislature that pledged to have separate schools for blacks and whites.

Daddy Dear was a music-loving man. His daughter never forgot their times together, checking out "people like Jimmie Lunceford, Basie, and Duke" when their bands played a hall in her hometown. Her dad stood "by the window with me on his shoulder, and that's the way I got turned on to this particular kind of music. At that time it was swing." Clora stayed tuned in to that music via radio broadcasts of big band shows.

When the draft took Clora's big brother, Fred, away in 1941, she took a shine to the trumpet he left behind. "My dad wanted me to play the harp, but I knew the trumpet was it."

Clora hit it, hit it, hit it—teaching herself scales.

Clora hit it, hit it, hit it—making it onto Terrell High's marching band and its faculty-student swing band.

This gal with a horn also hit the books. Senior year, Clora had scholarships to two colleges: one in the Midwest (Oberlin), the other in the South (Bennett). She passed on both when the chance to attend Prairie View came along.

An early Prairie View Co-Ed, alto sax player Bert Etta Davis, a native of San Antonio. In 1940, during her first year at Prairie View, she was bold enough to audition for the school's all-guy dance band—and was so good that musical director Will Bennett gave her a spot. But the dean of women snapped her cap—Oh, no, young lady!

**from the
Pittsburgh Courier:
March 11, 1944**

The absence of millions of men [has] left vacancies in many fields which are rapidly being filled by the fairer sex. At PV, in order that music may still be kept alive, the co-eds have taken over the horns and strings with tremendous success.

• • • • • • • • • • • • • • •

The *Pittsburgh Courier* was one of the most widely read black-owned newspapers.

Prairie View had once boasted not only a concert band and a marching band but also a scintillating all-guy dance band, the Collegians. The draft's drain on that band prompted musical director Will Bennett to create a draft-proof band in early 1943. He recruited girls from the school's music department and from its concert and marching bands. Presto change-o!—the Prairie View State College Co-Eds.

Will Bennett went on a talent search at Terrell High because he had friends there who could give him the straight dope on students with potential. Clora wasn't the only Terrell talent he scooped up. Another trumpeter, Elizabeth Thomas, and drummer Helen Cole also became Prairie View Co-Eds. The thrill of playing dance music in an all-girl band wasn't the only draw. The scholarship was a powerful lure. Helen spoke for many of her bandmates when she remarked years later that drumming with the Co-Eds was "the *only* way that I had of trying to put myself through school."

Count Basie's "Jumpin' at the Woodside," Harry James's "Back Beat Boogie," and Woody Herman's "At the Wood-choppers' Ball" were some of the hits the Co-Eds served up as they moved up from playing only on campus to playing clubs around the Lone Star State and at military bases—but only on the weekends. They *were* students, after all.

The band eventually came into wider view through bookings at Houston's Civic Auditorium. They played between main attractions, such as Cootie Williams's ork and Ella Fitzgerald, "First Lady of Swing."

"When school closes in June, do you think the girls will relax and go vacationing?" teased the *Prairie View Bulletin* in the spring of 1944.

Answer: "Not these super-energetic collegians. They plan to tour the entire country, playing at camps, bases, and dance dates."

The Co-Eds went on tour in the summer of 1944 under the aegis of the Big Apple–based booker Moe Gale. His

Mo' from Moe

Eddie Durham with his All-Star Girl Orchestra, also repped by Moe Gale's agency. "These were musicians with reflexibility and phrasing and volume and pianissimos and everything," Durham said of the All-Stars years later. Many of the chicks had played with the Harlem Playgirls and other all-girl orks that got around in the 1930s. Durham, a pioneer of the electric jazz guitar and ex-tramster and belly-fiddler for several topflight bands, was an ace composer and arranger, suiting up tunes for a host of bands, including Ina Ray Hutton's and Artie Shaw's. Durham's clefs include "Moten Swing," "Sliphorn Jive," "One O'Clock Jump," "Jumpin' at the Woodside," "Swingin' the Blues," "I Don't Want to Set the World on Fire," and "Wham! (Re Bop Boom Bam)." He was the arranger for the Glenn Miller Band's 1939 killer-diller cut of "In the Mood."

agency repped a cavalcade of greats, including Cab Calloway, the Ink Spots, Ella Fitzgerald, and Chick Webb. Moe also had a stake in the club that featured Webb's hard-driving ork as its house band: Harlem's Savoy Ballroom, birthplace, as legend has it, of the Lindy Hop, with its floor steps, shine steps, and air steps. The Savoy's nickname: "Home of Happy Feet."

In a Gale Agency "Publicity and Exploitation" tip sheet, the Co-Eds were called an "outstanding attraction" and "a seldom-found combination of true talent and rhythm that has proved a 'natural' to sell to the public." The item went on to boast that the Co-Eds "'give out' with that oomph that has put them in a class by themselves as the rave and rage of theatre, nite club and ballroom audiences!" Prompts from another promo piece on how a venue can sell out a Co-Eds concert included: "Place pictures in Beauty Parlors"; "Have your local florist designate a floral bouquet as 'the Prairie

The Co-Eds would one day play in Tuskegee, Alabama, for some of the army's first black flyboys. Here, Tuskegee Airmen stand before a P-40 Warhawk fighter.

During their tour, the Co-Eds hit several top venues that catered to blacks, including Balto's Royal and D.C.'s Howard theaters. Wherever they went, "we showed that women could play jazz," remembered Margaret Grigsby, who had played trombone at her high school in Houston.

View Bouquet,' with a photo of the Co-Eds shown"; "Music Stores will display photographs of the All-Girl Band . . . and the girls will gladly autograph pictures and endorse instruments"; and "Radio Interviews, Newspaper Tie-Ups, Autograph Parties and a Press Party can all be part of your campaign."

The Co-Eds didn't truly tour the "entire country," as their school newspaper bragged, but they most definitely put in some mileage—"from Texas up to Louisiana, on over to Florida and then up through Virginia, West Virginia, the Carolinas, Tennessee, Alabama, Mississippi," recalled Clora Bryant. "We played all the way up to New York."

"We played for fifteen thousand soldiers at Camp Lee, Virginia, just a sea of faces," remembered Bettye Bradley. Bettye's mom had her heart set on her daughter becoming a concert pianist, playing the likes of Beethoven, not music with a driving beat. When Bettye, a native of Alto, Texas, joined the Co-Eds, she was hot to play the alto sax, but

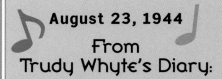

August 23, 1944

From Trudy Whyte's Diary:

About 1 AM bought 22 gal gas ($4.00). After that 35 mi before Bloomington, Ill. had burst tire. Removed by trucker ($1.00) and replace by spare . . . 3 mi before Decatur, Ill 2 rear blew out.

● ● ● ● ● ● ● ● ● ● ● ● ● ●

Trudy played trombone in her husband's all-white, all-girl ork, Virgil Whyte's Musical Sweethearts. When Virgil, a drummer, was drafted, his sister Alice, also a drummer, led the band.

Legendary Lindy Hoppers Willa Mae Ricker and Leon James take-off. Lindy Hoppers gave out lots of spins, slides, splits, breakaways, swing-outs—and plenty of jump. When this photo ran in Life *in 1943, it was captioned* "IMPROVISATION."

Bennett switched her to tenor. Bettye Boo's attitude about the switcheroo? *Reet!*

When Margaret Grigsby recalled a Co-Ed concert for black soldiers at another base, she remembered more than a "sea of faces." She remembered guys "up in trees! And, when we started playing, they turned loose and fell out of the trees. They yelled, *'That's* what *I'm* fighting for!' "

After the band's finale, for the sake of the girls' safety, "they had all these sergeants lined up, and the army truck, and they passed us hand over hand, the sergeants did, to keep us from getting down on the ground. . . . And they just passed us hand over hand and put us on the truck and took us out of there." It doesn't appear that the Co-Eds experienced a similar exit when they played for the Tuskegee Airmen.

The Prairie View crew traveled in a trio of station wagons. That was certainly a lot easier and more liberating than traveling by public transportation, but was not without its stresses. The Co-Eds kept their fingers crossed against flat tires. With the wartime rubber shortage, they were riding on cheapo synthetic ones like lots of other folks.

Fear of flat tires wasn't the only worry for the Co-Eds. They also had to contend with the cramp of Jim Crow. For black entertainers, landing in a town lacking a black-owned restaurant meant takeout from an eatery's back door, or taking off for a grocery store for the likes of soda crackers and tinned meat (maybe Armour's Treet) and other foodstuffs

Double V

"Double V" became the battle cry for the civil rights crusade during the war after a letter from James Thompson, a cafeteria worker at aircraft manufacturer Cessna, appeared in an early 1942 issue of the *Pittsburgh Courier.* Thompson's letter read, in part:

Being an American of dark complexion . . . these questions flash through my mind: "Should I sacrifice my life to live half American?" . . . "Is the kind of America I know worth defending?" "Will America be a true and pure democracy after this war?"

. . . The V for victory sign is being displayed prominently in all so-called democratic countries. . . . [L]et we colored Americans adopt the double VV for a double victory. The first V for victory over our enemies from without, the second V for victory over our enemies from within. For surely those who perpetuate these ugly prejudices here are seeking to destroy our democratic form of government just as surely as the Axis forces.

• • • • • • • • • • • • • • • • •

The *Pittsburgh Courier* did more than publish Thompson's letter. "In the next weekly issue of the *Courier* on February 7, four Double V drawings appeared [and] a Double V campaign was announced a week later on the front page," reported Patrick Washburn in his book about the black press during WWII.

Prairie View Co-Eds with musical director Will Bennett in the spotlight. Behind him (left to right): Nelda McElroy, Bobby Jean Nunn, Melvia Wrenn, Bert Etta Davis, Flores Jean Davis, Clora Bryant, Ernest Mae Crafton, Bernice Payne, Argie Mae Edwards, Marcella Gauthier, and Marion Bridges. Back row (left to right): Elizabeth Thomas, Jewel Simmons, Margaret Grigsby, Helen Cole, and Doretha Williams.

that made for quick-and-easy meals to eat by the side of the road. In a town without a hotel or boardinghouse that accepted black patrons, they had to make do with sleeping in their cars or buses if they hadn't found a family able to put them up for a night. (Some superstars had private railroad cars.) All this, to follow their bliss.

While the Prairie View Co-Eds made their way up to New York, they did so with hearts afire about playing at the famed Apollo. (As they neared the city, three tires blew.)

During their ten-day stay in New York, the band played between showings of films and variety shows, which featured exotic dancers, comedy acts, and vocal groups like the Cats and the Fiddle, with the Co-Eds hitting it last and being a smash! Standout moments include Clora Bryant taking off on Harry James's energetic gasser "Back Beat Boogie."

Standout memories include being rehearsed by famed

pianist and composer Eubie Blake and by Lucky Millinder, leader of a wildly popular band. The Co-Eds were absolutely jazzed about just being in the Big Apple, the city that even back then didn't seem to sleep.

Some of the Co-Eds also didn't sleep when they were supposed to. When they were sure their chaperone, Mrs. Von Charlton, was deep into her zzz's, the young adventurers tiptoed out into the night to catch music at area clubs. They dropped in on jam sessions, too, and did more than listen.

Ernest "Ernie" Mae Crafton with her baritone sax, backstage at the Apollo, July 1945. She had wanted to be a bandleader since age eleven, when she saw an all-girl band play in her hometown of Austin, Texas. After the show, Ernie had a chance to play the piano for the band's founder. He wanted her to transfer to his school so she could play in its all-girl band, but her mom said N-O. That band was the International Sweethearts of Rhythm.

"Oh, no, I played. We played," remembered Helen Cole. "You know, sometimes the guys were a little leery of girls playing drums. But I think they kind of respected me a little bit because they would let me sit in."

The Co-Eds' first time at the Apollo was not their last. They enjoyed encore performances there in the summers of 1945 and 1946. And the memories would linger on.

W hen the Prairie View Co-Eds made their debut at the Apollo in 1944, the International Sweethearts of Rhythm had been there, done that. This multi-culti musical corps was grooving high as the era's most celebrated all-girl band.

"What Are We Gonna Do for a Drummer?"
THE INTERNATIONAL SWEETHEARTS OF RHYTHM

Poster for a 1946 movie short, out of which came the one-song Soundie Jump Children.

The Sweethearts came out of the Magnolia State, from Piney Woods Country Life School (near Jackson), founded in 1909 by Laurence Clifton Jones. Though the boarding school was started with poor black children in mind, all you had to be to get in was eager to learn and willing to work. Students could pay for their education with their labor, from sowing and reaping to carpentry and basket weaving.

One way Piney Woods raised money was by booking its musical groups for religious and civic functions. The school had several "blossom" choirs—Cotton Blossoms, Magnolia Blossoms, Orange Blossoms. There was also an all-guy band, the Syncollegians, that served up jazz. In 1937, Laurence Jones seized upon the idea of the all-girl swing band, which became the International Sweethearts of Rhythm. Consuela Carter, Piney Woods alum and former Cotton Blossom turned faculty member, was the one who whipped the band into shape, teaching every instrument.

Early Sweethearts included Nina de La Cruz, Nova Lee McGee, and Alma Cortez, identified as Indian, Hawaiian, and Mexican, respectively. Some Sweethearts who were identified as something other than black actually had one black parent. When it came to choosing black members, Laurence Jones preferred light-skinned girls.

One teen who fit that bill was Helen "T.D." Jones, adopted daughter of Jones and his wife, Grace. Helen balked at Mr. Jones's idea that she play the violin and

The Sweethearts' sax choir, 1942. Standing (left to right): part–Native American, part-black Marjorie "Marge" Pettiford, lead sax. She had grown up playing in her father's band along with her brother, who achieved greater fame, bass player and cellist Oscar Pettiford. Beside Marge, Helen Saine and Amy Garrison. Seated (left): Grace Bayron (a Big Apple–born Puerto Rican, whose sister, Judy, played trams). Opposite Grace: Willie Mae Wong. Laurence Jones had recruited her from a largely black high school in Greenville, Mississippi. He didn't care that she didn't know squat about music. He wanted her face. To stress her Chinese ancestry, he changed her last name from Lee to Wong.

The Sweethearts' rhythm section, with Mendenhall, Mississippi–born Pauline Braddy definitely on the upbeat. (While on the road, she had the benefit of tutorials from legendary skinmen. One was "Papa" Jo Jones with Basie's band.) On doghouse, Lucille Dixon, who had played with New York City's All-City High School Orchestra and studied with the Philharmonic's Fred Zimmerman. On belly-fiddle, Roxanna Lucas. In the background (left), Johnnie Mae Rice, who did most of her swingcopating on the 88's.

begged to play trombone because she "loved to watch that slide going in and out." In the end, Helen had her way.

Almost out the gate, the Sweethearts played venues as varied as Wiley College in Marshall, Texas, and American Beach, a black-owned resort in Jacksonville, Florida. In time, the band played up-south hot spots, including Chicago's Regal and Detroit's Graystone.

"We rehearsed practically every day," remembered clarinetist turned alto sax player Helen Saine, from Bolivar, Tennessee. "We would get into a town twelve o'clock in the day, and we would probably have a rehearsal at two, from two to four, then play, say, from eight to twelve or nine until one."

The Sweethearts traveled in their "Hi-Way Home": a thirty-foot-long, eight-foot-wide semitrailer renovated and revamped by Piney Woods students. "The vehicle included Pullman beds for the Sweethearts and their chaperone, lavatory facilities, dressing and makeup rooms, kitchenette, three clothes closets, and cabinet drawers for each girl," wrote D. Antoinette Handy in her history of the band. "There was space for all of the instruments as well as a practice piano. There were studio couches and boudoir chairs such as those found in railroad observation cars." The chaperone was Rae Lee Jones (no relation to Piney Woods founder Laurence Jones).

As the Sweethearts went national in their Hi-Way Home, accolades accumulated. The *Chicago Defender* paid

Five Sweethearts flashing a little Suzy Q. Far right, vocalist Evelyn McGee (sometimes "McGhee" in the press), who fronted the band early on. One writer's praise for Evelyn: "One of the few singers in the world who has learned the secret of literally pouring herself into the mike."

trumpeter Edna Williams the ultimate compliment when it likened her playing to Louie Armstrong's. Call Edna "Miss Satchmo," the newspaper said. Edna, who also sang and played accordion, doubled as the band's musical director on the road.

"Mrs. Satchmo" (The Second)

Louie Armstrong's second wife was pianist, composer, arranger, and singer Lil Hardin. Lil and Louie married in 1924 when both were with King Oliver's Creole Jazz Band. By then, Lil had played in Chicago-based bands, briefly led a band of her own, and appeared in stage musicals, among them Eubie Blake and Noble Sissle's smash hit *Shuffle Along*. Lil is credited with giving Satchmo the gumption to quit King Oliver and start his own band. When Satchmo did, Lil was composer and piano player on several songs recorded by his early bands. Along with playing beside her man, Lil headed up several groups assembled for recording only. One was Lil's Hot Shots.

Lil Hardin Armstrong. After she and Louie split up, Lil kept her swing—on the bandstand, fronting Lil Armstrong's All-Girl Orchestra; on shellac, recording for Decca; and later as a solo nightclub act.

Satchmo's ork was the first big band the Sweethearts' drummer Pauline Braddy remembered seeing as a kid—"when Professor Jones took a bunch of the girls to Memphis, Tennessee," to see Armstrong. And it was a horn to which Pauline was first drawn. She was dead set on playing alto sax forever and a day. But she was basically trapped into traps. "They always said I had a good sense of rhythm. When the drummer that they had dropped out, they said, 'What are we gonna do for a drummer?' They said, 'Pauline's a natural.'"

Pauline's reaction? "I cried."

She made the most of the hand dealt to her, learning to roll, flam, triple paradiddle, flamadiddle, and other drum rudiments. Being dubbed "Queen of the Drums" was part of the payoff. The *Chicago Defender* contended that "this young swing drummer is one of the reasons why the International Sweethearts of Rhythm is by far the most popular girls' orchestra in the country today."

In late summer 1940, the Sweethearts placed third in a *Swing* magazine big band competition. Theirs was the only chick outfit among the thirty contestants. The event took place in Queens, New York, at the 1939–1940 World's Fair, where RCA unveiled its television and Westinghouse showcased its walking, talking robot, Elektro. The fair's theme: "Building the World of Tomorrow." In April 1941, the Sweethearts were building their tomorrows without Piney Woods.

"Girls' Band Flees Dixie After Tiff with School" read

the headline of an article in the D.C.-based *Afro-American*. "The girls who had been traveling for three years under the sponsorship of the Piney Woods School of Mississippi, playing dance dates and sending the funds back for the support of the school, severed their ties."

The *Afro-American* reported that the girls received "only $2 a week wages and fifty cents a day traveling expenses . . . and returned thousands of dollars to the school." In a follow-up story, the newspaper described the band's getaway— "pursued by highway police . . . through seven states to Washington and freedom." The seventeen Sweethearts on

A future Sweetheart crew, 1942. Taking it from the top (left to right): Marian Carter (trumpet), Marge Pettiford, Pauline Braddy, Johnnie Mae "Tex" Stansbury (trumpet), Amy Garrison, Judy Bayron, Lucille Dixon, Roxanna Lucas, and Johnnie Mae Rice. Middle: Helen Jones, Evelyn McGee, and Helen Saine. Bottom: Edna Williams, Ina Belle Byrd (trams), Anna Mae Winburn, Grace Bayron, and Willie Mae Wong. A succession of dynamite arrangers/musical directors were critical to the band's success. First, Eddie Durham. It was after he left the Sweethearts that he started the All-Stars, taking a few Sweethearts along. After Eddie, the Sweethearts had the benefit of composer-bandleader Jesse Stone, whom Evelyn McGee later married.

the run included Helen Jones, adopted daughter of Piney Woods' founder.

The split became the subject of heated debate. Some maintained that the Sweethearts were fed up with being financially exploited. Others that the girls were ingrates. The Sweethearts also charged that Piney Woods had pulled the plug on several girls' graduations to keep them in the band another year. (As it turned out, the girls' schooling was skimpy because they were on the road so much. The tutor that traveled with them was apparently window dressing.) Anyone who bet money on a reconciliation between the school and the band lost. For the Sweethearts, there was no turning back. They were gone for good. (Piney Woods didn't miss too many beats: the understudy band filled the void as the Swinging Rays of Rhythm.)

The Sweethearts' chaperone, Rae Lee Jones, had been in on the break—the instigator, some maintained—and became the band's manager. She brought in two investors about whom little is known.

The band's new home base was in Arlington, Virginia, a stone's throw from the training camp of boxer Joe Louis, aka the "Brown Bomber," world heavyweight champion since 1937. In this "Sweetheart House," a swell brick two-story at 908 South Quinn Street, the band practiced for sometimes six or more hours a day as they prepped to take-off anew.

When the new and improved International

Sweethearts of Rhythm made its debut at Howard Theatre in late summer 1941, the *New York Age* had this to say: "Truly amazing was the anxious throngs of rabid jitterbugs and staid old timers who waited for hours before show time, forming long lines extending for more

The Competition

After the Darlings of Rhythm came on the scene in 1943, some jazz fans felt that it bested the Sweethearts musicwise. Appearance was another matter. The Darlings didn't give a flam about glam. "We had a red coat with a black skirt and a white blouse. Then we had another one with a checked jacket with a white blouse," remembered the Darlings' bass player Vi Wilson, an ex-Sweetheart. "But the Sweethearts had all these beautiful gowns, short dresses and all, and they were fabulous with makeup and all . . . we just had what we had. But we could play." (Vi Wilson left the Sweethearts when a cousin who played in the black WAC band joined the Darlings.)

from *Metronome:*
March 1944

Apollo, New York.

This is still the best-looking band around, and still, alas, the furthest off-pitch. For all its faults, though, it rocks once in a while, and the girl trombonists really can get the house jumping with their "Three Bones" number. In fact, the whole brass team plays well on this.

Unluckily the band's two major talents, guitarist Roxanna Lucas and vocalist Anna Mae Winburn, weren't properly featured at the show . . .

Anna Mae, who conducts the band slinkily and looks terrific, had a cold and didn't sing.

Best spot in the show was the blues ad libbing behind one of the acts, Richard Huey, whose "Blues Boogie Woogie" was a sender. Second best, a chick named Vie Burnside taking a tenor solo on "Lady Be Good." Worst spot, a huge trumpet-blowing dame called Tiny Davis who sang the blues badly and put on a revolting exhibition.

This review was headlined "SWEETHEARTS OF RHYTHM: *Without Anna-mation.*" The scribe: Leonard Feather, an influential jazz critic.

than a block, in all kinds of weather and at every performance. . . . Once inside, things began to rock! The 'Hep Cats' began to jump and the Jitterbugs began to 'Jitter' as the Sweethearts began to romp!" The Sweethearts were part of an all-female revue. Billie Holiday topped the bill.

In mid-September, the band played the Apollo. Next stop, the Savoy. At the top of 1942—back at the Apollo in another all-female revue, and ever more determined "to be appreciated for their musical ability," reported Nell Dodson in the *Jackson Advocate.* The journalist added, "with the war and the draft threatening to deplete the ranks of men musicians, the International Sweethearts of Rhythm may find themselves in the big money class very soon, and so in anticipation they are preparing themselves to blow as long, loud and fine as any of the others." The big money class? At a time when some topflight big bands brought in more than 100,000 bills a year, the Sweethearts grossed about 25K.

"Sweethearts to 'Battle' Smack Henderson Soon" read the headline of an item in the April 1, 1942, issue of the *Beat.* "The Sweethearts of Rhythm, girding themselves for the musical battle of the sexes which sets them against Fletcher Henderson's bunch starting April 5, made an important addition to their personnel here when Jean Starr was added to the trumpet section," the article began.

TWO MORE BANDS IN SERVICE

CHICAGO, DECEMBER 1, 1942   Vol. 9—No. 23

Merchant Marine Gets
Phil Harris, Ted Weems
And Both Their Bands

By summer 1942, many bandleaders had lost a quarter or more of their sidemen to Uncle Sam. The "Band Leaders' Honor Roll" column in an April 1943 issue of the Beat *listed the names of a little over sixty male bandleaders in the military. Four months later, the Honor Roll had doubled.*

Fletcher Henderson, innovator of big band arrangements, was called "Smack" because he liked to smack his lips while playing the 88's. As for Jean Starr, she was in and out of the Sweethearts a few times.

This same *Beat* article noted, "vocalist Anna Mae Winburn is now handling the baton." Anna Mae, born in Port Royal, Tennessee, had been working her talents (singing, dancing, belly-fiddle playing) since she was a teen, after her mother died, and she put her younger sibs "around in different families" (by then, her family was living in Indiana). For Anna Mae, surviving included passing as a Spaniard named Anita Door at one point— "If I passed for Spanish, I could get more work." She also fronted several bands, including the K.C. Blue Devils, reconstituted as her Cotton Club Boys. (One of those boys was the great guitarist Charlie Christian, an Eddie Durham protégé.)

As for the "battle" between the Sweethearts and Smack's band—hype. It was simply a tour. The two

Anna Mae Winburn joined the Sweethearts shortly after they made their great escape.

One of the few 78's the Sweethearts recorded.

bands "played alternate sets and combined in a 35-piece arrangement for the finale," explains jazz historian Rosetta Reitz.

While touring with Smack and after that, the Sweethearts kept blowing swingsters away around the nation, with a return engagement at the Apollo in May 1942. This time they shared the bill with the all-boy harmony group the Charioteers, stars of the Broadway musical *Hellzapoppin'*.

And the Sweethearts kept poppin'.

A 1944 *DownBeat* poll ranked the Sweethearts "America's #1 All-Girl Orchestra." One of the reasons the band was so tight—it kept snagging top talents, from Marge Pettiford to Toby Butler, a white trumpet and bass player who joined the band in 1943. Toby, born in Richmond, Virginia, was raised by a black family since age seven, after her mother died. Her adoptive mom knew Rae Lee Jones.

Other tight talent to come included two ex–Harlem Playgirls. One was Viola "Vi" Burnside, renowned for her driving tenor sax (sometimes called "Vie" or "Vy" in the press). When the Sweethearts and the Darlings of Rhythm crossed paths, they sometimes had jam sessions, with showdowns between the star tenor saxes: the Sweethearts' Vi Burnside and the Darlings' "Padjo" (Margaret Backstrom), who had worked together in the Harlem Playgirls for two years. The other ex-Playgirl

BLENDING THE MUSICAL PATTERNS OF
THE FIVE CONTINENTS INTO SOLID RHYTHM
AND $OLID BOX OFFICE

INTERNATIONAL SWEETHEARTS OF RHYTHM

PUBLICITY
DANIEL M. GARY

FEATURING: ★ PAULINE BRADDY · VI BURNSIDE · TINY DAVIS
EXCLUSIVE MANAGEMENT: FREDERICKS BROTHERS AGENCY

An ad from Billboard*'s 1945–46 Music Year Book. One thing the Sweethearts never advertised was its white members. That could—and did— get the band run out of some towns. White Sweethearts often wore makeup darker than what they would normally use. One such musician, Toby Butler, is far right in the ad's trumpet patch. Another white member had played with Ada Leonard's ork: Rosalind "Roz" Cron, Beantown native (in the center of the sax choir). After Roz almost blew her cover in a Southern town, she was determined to do whatever she had to do—from being ever-vigilant about her racial p's and q's (like not trying to get a soda at whites-only lunch counters when with black bandmates) to dyeing "my face and hair"—if that's what it took to be with "the best" chick big band in the U.S. of A.*

who became a Sweetheart was Ernestine "Tiny" Davis, who billed herself as "245 Lbs. of Solid Jive and Rhythm." Tiny was known for her trumpet playing and her onstage antics.

One of the songs Vi and Tiny typically took off on

was Erskine Hawkins's hit "Tuxedo Junction," the Savoy Ballroom favorite and the most popular jazz tune of WWII. That tune and "Swing Shift" were two of the songs the Sweethearts performed on *Jubilee*, the Armed Forces Radio Service's weekly variety show created with black troops in mind (recorded in the States and shortwaved overseas). *Jubilee* broadcasts featured sensational songbirds such as Lena Horne and Ivie Anderson and outstanding

This montage is from the Sweethearts' time in Europe for the USO.

orks, including the Duke's, the Count's, and the bands of Lionel Hampton, Benny Carter, Andy Kirk, and Satchmo.

In the summer of 1945, the Sweethearts were packing their bags for a six-month tour through France and Germany to entertain troops. It was Band-on-Demand. GIs had been clamoring for Sweethearts camp shows.

"We get the best of everything. In camp we eat in the officers' mess and the food is fine," wrote Willie Mae Wong in a letter published in the *Chicago Defender.* Willie Mae shared highlights from the band's time in the City of

This July 1945 issue of the Beat *was the mag's first special edition for troops overseas. The cover girl was a member of the Coast Guard's SPARS, who "helps the public relations campaign of the SPARS by singing on several service radio shows."*

Bill Treadwell dedicated his Big Book of Swing *to the great Glenn Miller, one of the musicians who died overseas during the war. In 1942, Miller joined the Army Air Force, for which he raised a marching band, then a dance band. That band included several cats from Miller's civvie ork and singer Johnny Desmond.*

♪ **from the**
Nevada Journal:

YOKOHAMA, Wednesday, Jan. 23 (UP)—Sharon Rogers, the all-girl band leader who scolded American soldiers for fraternizing with Japanese girls, and 16 members of her troupe were rescued early today by Japanese fishermen after their army C-47 crashed into the sea off Kyushu. All occupants of the plane were saved, including the crew, but Gee Jay, of Chicago, the band's blond drummer, fractured her leg, and the other band members as well as the accompanying army officers were treated for shock and minor bruises.

•••••••••••••••••

The Sharon Rogers All-Girl Band grew out of the Melody Maids, a band Sharon and some Chi-Town high school friends formed in 1940. At the time of the plane crash, Sharon's band was on a USO tour of the Philippines, Korea, and Japan.

Lights, like playing Paris's Olympia Theatre, a show "broadcast to all servicemen who were unable to attend the performances."

The Sweethearts had only one regret, said Willie Mae: "that more Negro soldiers can't attend the various performances we give." Not true for the entire tour. They did play for black troops in Germany.

But being in that war-wrecked nation meant the girls didn't always have it plush—"to travel like soldiers, in those big old vans, with no food, eating K rations, sleeping on the floor sometimes. . . . I think it's worth mentioning," said Anna Mae Winburn in an interview years later.

On tour with the Sweethearts was their musical director since 1943, Maurice King. Like Eddie Durham and Jesse Stone before him, Maurice cared more about a chick's talent than her face. He also gave the band several of its top tunes, including "Vi Vigor," a rollicking romp with solos from Vi Burnside. He loved her playing and wrote songs to showcase her gifts. (Maurice would later work his mojo for Motown.) And thanks to him, each Sweetheart received her pay from the source—not from the manager. Up until then, they had been royally ripped off. When the band was in its glory days, the average Sweetheart received a mere fifteen bucks per gig, playing three gigs a week on average. These girls were told that money was being deducted from their pay for Social Security and for expenses, including the Sweetheart

House, property they thought they co-owned. Lies. All of it was lies, the Sweethearts later learned.

When the band took off for Europe, the war was winding down and America had a new president, Harry S. Truman. FDR died on April 12, 1945. On May 8, the Allies celebrated Victory in Europe Day, aka V-E Day. V-J Day came in August, after the atomic bombing of the Japanese cities Hiroshima and Nagasaki.

After returning to the States, the International Sweethearts of Rhythm continued to enjoy success, but in time, like other all-girl bands, it faded away.

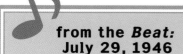

**from the *Beat:*
July 29, 1946**

New York—Toby Butler, a trumpet player with the Darlings of Rhythm, all-girl orchestra, recently was "detained by authorities when the band played Milledgeville, Georgia, and it was alleged that Toby was a white girl and her association with other members of the band was prohibited in the state of Georgia."

• • • • • • • • • • • • • • •

The ex-Sweetheart didn't end up in a Georgia slammer because the Darlings' leader, the light-skinned Jessie Turner, convinced the police that Toby was her cousin. Jessie later told the press, "I don't see that it would matter even if there were a few women from Mars mixed in." Jessie stressed that she was all about creating "the best musical unit possible."

Outro ★

**GIRL MUSICIANS.
ALL INSTRUMENTS:**
**Steady work, pay for rehearsals. Chance
to travel with the Marching Swing Band.
Must be young and between
five feet two and five feet six inches tall.**

This was the start of a late July 1946 help-wanted ad placed by George "Red" Bird. He had organized Massillon Washington High's Tiger Swing Band in the late 1930s. He was now with a pro football team: the Cleveland Browns. The ad's silence on the talent requirement suggests that Bird's interest in fems with skills was nil.

A sign of the times.

When the war ended, millions of men in the military were eager, understandably, to get back to jobs on the home front. Propagandists flipped the script. For many women, the new norm was the old norm: a woman's place was in the home—not in a plant, or behind the wheel of a truck, and not on a bandstand laying down the righteous jive.

Though many women remained in the workforce— especially low-income women who had always worked— most gals got sacked from their "hard, masculine" jobs.

Drafted in 1942, piano player/composer Mel Powell landed in Glenn Miller's Army Air Force Band. One of the tunes Mel came up with while overseas became the 1945 hit "My Guy's Come Back."

THE GUY'S COME BACK!

Some were limited to domestic work. Others, to playing the office piano (typewriter).

Women with a beat?

With cats among the ranks of the mustered out, many joints felt it only right to give guys the first shot at gigs.

Ada Leonard with her smaller band, 1952. Reed section (left to right): Evelyn Pennak, Helen Ireland, Marge Stafford, Evie Campbell, and Peggy Gilbert. Behind them (left to right): bass player and vocalist Mildred Springer, trumpet players Francis Rossiter, Helen Hammond, and Dorothy Lilley, and tramster Lois Cronin. On drums: Margaret Ewing. In 1955, Ada switched to batoning an all-boy band.

Janie Sager lost her job doing studio work for CBS. "Janie, I've got to let you go," the bossman said. When she asked why, he replied, "They're coming back from the service, and they've got families." She pointed out that she, too, had a family, but to no avail.

While many Janies were getting the brush-off, some fem cats took themselves out of play. Being a musician had never been their everything. Prairie View Co-Ed tramster Margaret Grigsby had her sights set on being a doctor. After college, she went to the University of Michigan Medical School. "I put the horn down in 1944, and I never picked it up again."

There were Joans, Sharons, Connies, Jeans, and Ediths who hung up their neck straps, packed away their drum kits, and stashed trams and trumpets in trunks because they were simply road-weary, discrimination-weary. Others wanted to marry and have children, and couldn't see a way to make band and family mix. Sherrie Tucker tells of a vet who took his wife's band memorabilia into their backyard and torched her memories: "Also a musician, and jealous that his wife had occupied the bandstand while he was in combat, he destroyed the objects that would remind her of her career."

Some lassies stayed in the business. Ada Leonard trimmed her ork after the war and even had a TV show (1952–1954). Duke Ellington's "Sophisticated Lady" was her theme song.

Ina Ray Hutton also had a show, for a flash (summer 1956). She had been back on the block with an all-girl ork since the early 1950s, one in which Janie Sager did a stint. "Five Foot Two, Eyes of Blue (Has Anybody Seen My Gal?)" was Ina's theme song.

The Prairie View Co-Eds were over by late 1946. The International Sweethearts of Rhythm disbanded a few

The cover of Clora Bryant's 1957 album. Over the years, Clora played with a variety of bands, some all-chick, some not, and one of her own: Swi-Bop. She was quite instrumental in L.A.'s Central Avenue sounds, and this gal with a horn continued to play until the mid-1990s. In 2002, when she was in her mid-seventies, she received the Kennedy Center's Mary Lou Williams Women in Jazz Award, named for the pioneering jazz musician, composer, and arranger who was 88'ing for a buck an hour in 1916 at age six.

years later. For a while, Anna Mae Winburn fronted a "Sweethearts" band, but with the "International" nixed and Norma Carson from Ada's first band in the mix.

After Phil Spitalny closed the curtain on the Hour of Charm in 1954, Viola Smith stayed on the scene for about twenty years with a solo act, billed as "Viola Smith and Her Seventeen Drums." Another drummer, Helen Cole, along with fellow Prairie View Co-Eds alumna Bert Etta Davis, was part of a sextet that morphed into a combo headed up by an ex-Sweetheart horn player: Tiny Davis's Hell-Divers. Yet another chick hot with the sticks, Fagel Liebman, was with Flo Dryer combos for many years. Another former

Co-Ed, Ernie Mae Crafton, became a solo act, only she switched from that big baritone sax to piano, her first instrument.

Solos, duos, trios, quartets, quintets, sextets—that's where many ex–big band chicks ended up. Not because they were women, but because big bands fell out of fashion. Causes include the closure of many ballrooms and other grand spaces, new entertainment taxes, and an uptick in the cost of lodging and transportation. Live jazz still sold, but by the late 1940s it was no big thing if it did not have that swing. A new jazz prime for small bands was making waves, with Charlie Parker, Dizzy Gillespie, and Oscar Pettiford among its pioneers—re-bop, or be-bop, or simply bop! What's more, rhythm and blues was catching the groove of bookoo dance fanatics.

Few members of all-girl bands during WWII left accounts of their days (and nights) on the bandstand. Not many were the subjects of oral history projects. The Swinghearts, Lorraine Page and Her Orchestra, the Platinum Blondes of America, 'Stelle Slavin and Her Brunettes, Betty McGuire's Sub-Debs, Joan Lee and Her Girl Orchestra, the Dixie Rhythm Girls, the Dixie Sweethearts, the Harlem Playgirls, the Fourteen Bricktops, the Sepia Lassies of Harmony, Eleanor Ten and Her Smoothies, Anna Jones's Western Swing Girls, the Darlings of Rhythm, the Daughters of Uncle Sam—there are scores of all-girl orks that popped up during WWII and before.

Clora Bryant (age 67) and Janie Sager (a few days after turning 80) in L.A., June 10, 1994. Sherrie Tucker took this photo when she was interviewing them for her book Swing Shift. *Had it not been for Jim Crow, Clora and Janie might have played their horns in the same brass section during WWII. Each had been a fan of the other's talent. On that June day in 1994, they were so thrilled to see each other—and to hear the other's stories. Sherrie swung into action with her camera right after Janie played an impromptu trumpet tribute to "my hero, Clora Bryant."*

But, sadly, most of their stories have been lost. So, too, their sound. Very few made shorts and Soundies. Very few waxed sides.

Post-war books on jazz ignored chick bands completely, or gave them cursory and usually condescending mention. Most famous (and infamous) is the damnation from former *Metronome* editor George Simon, whose column was called "Simon Sez." In his 1967 book, *The Big Bands,* Simon said of Ina Ray Hutton: "The early part of her career had been spent fronting an all-girl orchestra, one that most of us have forgotten and that she has probably been trying to forget ever since she gave it up to surround herself with men. For her all-girl orchestra was like all all-girl orchestras. 'Only God can make a tree,' I remember having written in a review of some other such outfit, 'and only men can play good jazz.' "

Oh, no, Daddy-o, historians, mostly women, countered in years to come. They produced articles, books, lectures, and documentaries that put the spotlight on groups like Ada Leonard's All-American Girl Orchestra, the Prairie View State College Co-Eds, and the International Sweethearts of Rhythm. Thanks to chicks with a pen and a lens, in the late twentieth century, interest in early all-girl bands began to take-off.

GLOSSARY

BLUES: A black folk music rooted in work songs and spirituals and characterized by its secular content and simple, repetitive musical structure.

BOOGIE-WOOGIE: A lively piano-based blues style that focused on up-tempo arrangements especially suited for dancing.

BOP: A very rhythmically and harmonically complex type of jazz. Distinguishing features include the flattened fifth.

CHOPS: Skills.

CUT THE RUG (or CUT A RUG): To dance.

DOWNBEAT: A bandleader's downward stroke to mark the first beat of a measure. Also, the first beat of a measure.

DRIVING: Having an instrumental dexterity marked by great emotion. Describing up-tempo jazz arrangements that highlight a band's "tightness," or ability to play in time with each other.

GIG: A paying job.

HIDE-BEATER: A drummer, also known as a tubman and a skinman. "Skinbeater" was slang for both a drummer and drumsticks, and "skins" for drums.

HOT LICKS (or LICKS): Skillful and impassioned jazz solos or musical phrasings.

JAM: A brief bit of improvisation by an entire band during a performance. In a "jam session," musicians come together to play for themselves, accent on improvisation.

JAZZ: "Man, if you gotta ask, you'll never know," Louie Armstrong once quipped. At base, jazz is a gumbo of different African and European music traditions, which became prominent in New Orleans in the 1890s. Jazz features blue notes, polyrhythms, and improvisation.

JITTERBUG: A dance with jittery moves and fast steps, or a person who does such a dance, or a swing fan in general. Jitterbugs were also called alligators.

JIVE: A synonym for swing. "To jive" meant "to dance to swing music." The word also came to connote dishonesty and deception.

JUMP: A synonym for up-tempo swing. "To jump" meant "to have a good time," thus such songs as Count Basie's "One O'Clock Jump" and "Jumpin' at the Woodside," Fats Waller's "This Joint Is Jumpin'," and the Louis Prima hit "Jump, Jive an' Wail."

LINDY HOP: A fusion of the Charleston and other dances created by blacks in the 1920s.

PLATTER: A record, also known as a side, a cut, and a disc.

RAGTIME: The earliest form of what would become known as jazz music, this piano-based precursor to jazz was noted for its "ragged time" and the virtuosity of its players such as Scott Joplin.

REET: All right, okay, or excellent.

RHYTHM AND BLUES: A blend of the blues and jazz introduced in the 1940s by practitioners such as pianist and vocalist Charles Brown and saxophonist and vocalist Louis Jordan. Jordan's 1946 hit "Let the Good Times Roll" is a classic example of an old-school rhythm-and-blues tune. Out of rhythm and blues came rock and roll and soul music.

RIDE CYMBAL: The cymbal that serves to maintain rhythm as opposed to making accents as with the hi-hat and crash cymbals. "Ride" was slang for rhythm.

RIFF: A two- or four-bar musical phrase. The interpolation of a fragment of a usually well-known tune into another musical arrangement. A repeated phrase, usually played by the horn section. Also, to speak.

RIGHTEOUS: Excellent.

SALTY: Angry.

SATCHMO: Short for "Satchelmouth," referring to the size of Louie Armstrong's mouth. Before Satchelmouth and then Satchmo stuck, he was called Gatemouth.

SCAT: A jazz vocal style identified by nonsensical melodic and rhythmic utterances.

SENDER: Someone or something that wows.

$64 QUESTION: A catchphrase for the biggest or most difficult question. In the 1940s radio quiz show *Take It or Leave It*, the correct answer to the last question earned a contestant sixty-four dollars. The show inspired the television game show *The $64,000 Question*.

SNAP YOUR CAP: Lose your cool.

SOUNDIE: A music video of the 1940s, played on a Panoram (a jukebox with a screen) for ten cents a pop.

SUZY-Q: A lively dance step featuring heel swivels.

SWEET: Describing a slower, less driving type of jazz.

SWING SHIFT: Usually the 4 pm–midnight work shift. The hours depend on the hours for the company's day and graveyard shifts. Many firms, especially those that produced war-related goods, started swing shifts for the first time during World War II.

WALKING BASS: A style of bass playing that relies on unsyncopated progressions or steps, used most notably in boogie-woogie music.

W. C. HANDY: Alabama-born composer and bandleader, self-promoted as the "father" of the blues. Handy helped to popularize the blues by annotating and publishing blues songs. His greatest hits include "Memphis Blues," "Beale Street Blues," and "St. Louis Blues."

WOODSHED (or SHED): Rigorous musical practice by musicians to improve their chops.

NOTES

Epigraph

Quotes from Treadwell and artists: *Big Book of Swing*, 8–10.

Intro

Help-wanted ad: *DownBeat*, June 15, 1941, 23.

"If I were . . .": Spitalny, quoted in *Swing Shift*, 81.

On "Apple": In his *Hepster's Dictionary*, Cab Calloway defined "Apple" as "the big town, the main stem, Harlem." (In the mid-1930s, a club called the Big Apple opened in Harlem on 135th Street and 7th Avenue.) Some jazzists nicknamed the cluster of clubs on West 52nd Street ("Swing Street") "the Apple." This was years after a columnist for a New York newspaper began referring to New York City as the Big Apple.

"Jitterbugs Jam James's . . .": *Life*, May 10, 1943, 34.

"Good jazz is . . ." and **"Women like violins . . .":** Marvin Freedman, "Here's the Lowdown on 'Two Kinds of Women,' " *DownBeat*, February 1, 1941, 9. The magazine's name was spelled *Down Beat* for most of its life. I use the current *DownBeat* in deference to the wishes of the magazine's publisher, Frank Alkyer.

On McKinney's Cotton Pickers: This black band was the Graystone's house band. Management stuck them with the demeaning name. The man who ran the Graystone (and co-created the Cotton Pickers) was Jean Goldkette, leader and promoter of several jazz bands in the 1920s and 1930s.

Early's comments: "White Noise and White Knights: Some Thoughts on Race, Jazz, and the White Jazz Musician," in *Jazz*, 324.

On Ina Ray Hutton: She was born Odessa Cowan and was known as the "Blonde Bombshell of Rhythm." Her best-known work with her all-guy band is in the film *Ever Since Venus*. Ina's younger sister, who took the name June Hutton, sang with her band, then for Charlie Spivak's, then with the vocal group the Pied Pipers.

"In some places . . .": *American Women in Jazz*, 96.

Part 1

On Ada Leonard: She made medical news in 1938 when she refused to have her ruptured appendix removed and instead chose a nonsurgical treatment that included ice packs and blood transfusions. One newspaper headlined a story about what was deemed her dicey decision: " 'Would Rather Die than Mar Beauty,' Says Strip Artist" (UP item in Wisconsin's *Sheboygan Press,* July 28, 1938, accessed at www.ancestry.com). Turns out, Ada was ahead of her time: today nonsurgical treatment of appendicitis is generally the preferred first option.

Sager's account of the Fort Belvoir show: *Swing Shift,* 274.

"I could play . . .": Sager, quoted in *American Women in Jazz,* 103.

On Rita Rio: Some sources say she was born Rita Novello in Mexico City; others Eunice Westmoreland (or Westmorelanda) in Miami.

Article on Leonard's band: "Strip-Tease Ada Leonard Fronts Ace Fem Outfit," *DownBeat,* June 15, 1941, 6.

On catcalls: *Swing Shift,* 260.

On eighty bucks: *Swing Shift,* 229, 284.

Tucker's reconstruction of a USO show: *Swing Shift,* 279.

Viola Smith's article: *DownBeat,* February 1, 1942, 8.

"the group was . . .": *Swing Shift,* 280.

"playing army camps . . .": "Leonard on Coast," *DownBeat,* April 1, 1942, 6.

Fossum's article: "Girls Shouldn't Play Too Much Jazz, Says Ada," *DownBeat,* December 1, 1942, 14.

On the Schmitz Sisters: The band changed its name at one point to the Smith Sisters, possibly because of the rising tide of anti-German sentiment.

Hudee's letter: *DownBeat,* April 1, 1942, 10.

"definitely on the jump . . ." and **"When the band . . .":** Music critics, quoted in *Swing Shift,* 281.

"The band was . . ." and **"unbelievable. It was . . ."**: Liebman, quoted in *American Women in Jazz*, 159.

"the first thing . . .": Sager, quoted in *American Women in Jazz*, 90.

"everyone's licks": Liebman, quoted in *American Women in Jazz*, 156.

"And when I . . . ," **"the first really . . . ,"** **"great arranger,"** and **"I only left . . ."**: Liebman, quoted in *American Women in Jazz*, 156, 158.

"As the band's *sound* . . .": *Swing Shift*, 283.

"these strange-lookin' . . ." and **"was murder. On . . ."**: Carson, quoted in *American Women in Jazz*, 165.

On Mercurochrome: "The Big Ban," 16.

On high heels and contact lenses: *Swing Shift*, 61–62.

On Joan Lee's band: *DownBeat*, June 15, 1943, 13.

Sager on Fred Harvey sandwiches: *Swing Shift*, 271.

"Boy, did I . . .": Sager, quoted in *Swing Shift*, 280.

Sager's encounter with amputee: *Swing Shift*, 278–79.

Article on Valaida Snow: Will Roland, "Trumpeter-Singer Valaida Snow Tells of Nazi Imprisonment," *Metronome*, May 1943, 8, 28.

FDR's letter: *Metronome*, May 1943, 9.

"more than proud . . .": "Rhythm and Romance," *Band Leaders*, November 1944, 47.

"I would have . . ." and **"Once on a . . ."**: Liebman, quoted in *American Women in Jazz*, 159.

Part 2

"I said, 'If . . .": Bryant, quoted in *Swing Shift*, 97.

"people like Jimmie . . . ," **"by the window . . . ,"** and **"My dad wanted . . ."**: Bryant, quoted in *American Women in Jazz*, 152.

Excerpt from the *Pittsburgh Courier* article: *Swing Shift*, 97.

"the *only* way . . .": Cole, quoted in *Swing Shift*, 110.

Quotes from the *Prairie View Bulletin:* *Swing Shift,* 117.

"These were musicians . . .": Durham, quoted in *American Women in Jazz,* 149.

Gale Agency publicity materials: miscellaneous items from the Special Collections/Archives, John B. Coleman Library, Prairie View A&M University, Prairie View, Texas.

"from Texas up . . ." and **"We played all . . .":** Bryant, quoted in *Swing Shift,* 121.

"We played for . . .": Bradley, quoted in *Swing Shift,* 125. (At the time of the interview, her name was Bettye Bradley Kimbrough.)

Excerpt from Trudy Whyte's diary: *Swing Shift,* 66.

"IMPROVISATION": *Life,* August 23, 1943, 103.

Grigsby's recollection of a concert for soldiers: *Swing Shift,* 122.

"we showed that . . .": Grigsby, quoted in "The Ladies of Jazz, Swing—and Beyond," posted at www.nfo.net/usa/females.html.

Thompson's letter and Washburn's comments: *A Question of Sedition,* 54–55.

"Oh, no, I . . .": Cole, quoted in *Swing Shift,* 128.

Part 3

Willie Mae Wong's parentage: *Swing Shift,* 191. Her father was Chinese and her mother was part Native American. She told Sherrie Tucker that she didn't remember her mother's full ancestry.

"loved to watch . . .": Helen Jones, quoted in *Marian McPartland's Jazz World,* 136.

"We rehearsed practically . . .": Saine, quoted in *American Women in Jazz,* 144.

Description of semitrailer: *The International Sweethearts of Rhythm,* 110.

***Chicago Defender* on Edna Williams:** *The International Sweethearts of Rhythm,* 109.

"One of the . . .": *Jackson Advocate,* quoted in *The International Sweethearts of Rhythm,* 151.

"when Professor Jones . . . ," **"They always said . . . ,"** and **"I cried"**: Braddy, quoted in *American Women in Jazz,* 135–36. (At the time of the interview, her name was Pauline Braddy Williams.)

"this young swing . . .": *Chicago Defender,* quoted in *The International Sweethearts of Rhythm,* 110.

Quotes from the *Afro-American:* *The International Sweethearts of Rhythm,* 127.

***New York Age* review:** *The International Sweethearts of Rhythm,* 150.

"We had a red . . .": Vi Wilson, quoted in *Swing Shift,* 208.

Feather's review: "Sweethearts of Rhythm *Without Anna-mation,*" *Metronome,* November 1944, 33.

Nell Dodson's remarks: *The International Sweethearts of Rhythm,* 154.

Article on the Sweethearts and Henderson's band: "Sweethearts to 'Battle' Smack Henderson Soon," *DownBeat,* April 1, 1942, 5.

Percentages of bands lost to military: *Swing Shift,* 16, 47–48.

"Band Leaders' Honor Rolls": *DownBeat,* April 15, 1943, 14, and August 1, 1943, 21.

"around in different . . ." and **"If I passed . . ."**: Winburn, quoted in *American Women in Jazz,* 146.

On Cron passing for black: *Swing Shift,* 152.

"played alternate sets . . .": Reitz, Liner Notes, *The International Sweethearts of Rhythm.*

Tiny Davis's billing: *Marian McPartland's Jazz World,* 132.

Willie Mae Wong's letter: Reprinted in *The International Sweethearts of Rhythm,* 164. (She later became Willie Mae Wong Scott.)

On woman on cover of *DownBeat:* "SPARS' Siren on the Cover," *DownBeat,* July 1, 1945, 1.

Article on plane crash: "All-Girl Orchestra's Plane Crashes Into Sea; Rescued by Jap Fisherman," *Nevada Journal,* January 23, 1946, 1. Sharon Rogers's band wasn't the only all-girl ork to face danger while overseas for the USO. A lightning strike forced the plane carrying Joy Cayler's band into an emergency landing on Iwo Jima. Al D'Artega's band lived to tell about a submarine attack in the Straits of Gibraltar.

"to travel like . . .": Winburn, quoted in *American Women in Jazz,* 133.

On money: *Swing Shift,* 56, and *The International Sweethearts of Rhythm,* 25.

Article on Toby Butler: Eddie Ronan, "Girl Trumpeter Tastes Southern Chivalry and Color Ousts Mab's Men," *DownBeat,* July 29, 1946, 1. "Mab's Men" refers to high-note trumpeters Al Killian and Paul Webster in the band of white saxman Charlie "The Mab" Barnet. Killian and Webster had played on the sound track for the Monogram movie *Freddie Steps Out.* When they showed up along with the rest of the band to shoot their scenes, Monogram bigwigs eighty-sixed them and snagged some white dudes as replacements. Asked for their instruments and uniforms, "the musickers, backed by Charlie, said no dice, or stronger words to that effect," reported the *Beat.*

Outro

Help-wanted ad: *DownBeat,* July 29, 1946, 19.

Sager's exchange with boss: *Swing Shift,* 320.

"I put the . . .": Grigsby, quoted in *Swing Shift,* 129.

On husband burning wife's memorabilia: *Swing Shift,* 321.

"The early part . . .": *The Big Bands,* 261.

On June 10, 1994, photo: E-mail from Sherrie Tucker to the author, July 9, 2006.

SELECTED SOURCES

Books, Articles, and Liner Notes

"Brass Beat History: Miss Joy Cayler—Queen of the Trumpet." Posted at www.brassbeat.org.

Cooper, Beverly C. "Viola Smith: Female Drummers of the Swing Era." *Not So Modern Drummer,* Summer 2002, 4–7.

Dahl, Linda. *Stormy Weather: The Music and Lives of a Century of Jazzwomen.* Pompton Plains, NJ: Amadeus Press/Limelight Editions, 2004.

Erenberg, Lewis A. *Swingin' the Dream: Big Band Jazz and the Rebirth of American Culture.* Chicago: University of Chicago Press, 1998.

Feather, Leonard. Liner Notes, *Girls in Jazz* (three-disc set). 78rpm. RCA Victor.

Gallert, Jim, with Lars Bjorn. "Maurice King: Music Master." Posted at www.detroitmusichistory.com.

Gates, David Alan. "The Big Ban: Women in Music—Not Just for the Boys!" *Overture* (organ of AFM Local 47), April 2005, 16–17.

Handy, D. Antoinette. *Black Women in American Bands and Orchestras.* 2nd ed. Lanham, MD: Scarecrow Press, 1998.

——. *The International Sweethearts of Rhythm: The Ladies Jazz Band from Piney Woods Country Life School.* Revised ed. Lanham, MD: Scarecrow Press, 1998.

——. "Mary Lou Williams: First Lady of the Jazz Keyboard." Posted at www.kennedy-center.org/programs/jazz/womeninjazz/1stlady.html.

Lingeman, Richard. *Don't You Know There's a War On? The American Home Front, 1941–1945.* New York: Thunder's Mouth Press/Nation Books, 2003.

"Lucille Dixon," in "Requiem" column of *Allegro* (organ of AFM Local 802), December 2004. Posted at www.local802afm.org/publication_entry.cfm?xEntry=391643#dixon.

McPartland, Marian. *Marian McPartland's Jazz World: All in Good Time.* Chicago: University of Illinois Press, 2003.

Milkowski, Bill. *Swing It! An Annotated History of Jive.* New York: Billboard Books, 2001.

Miller, Norma, with Evette Jensen. *Swingin' at the Savoy: The Memoir of a Jazz Dancer.* Philadelphia: Temple University Press, 1996.

Napoleon, Art. Liner Notes, *Women in Jazz: All Women Groups.* 33rpm. Stash Records, 1978.

Pfeffer, Murray. "The Ladies of Jazz, Swing—and Beyond." Posted at www.nfo.net/usa/females.html.

Placksin, Sally. *American Women in Jazz: 1900 to the Present.* Los Angeles: Wideview Books/PEI Books, 1982.

Pool, Jeannie. "The Peggy Gilbert Story: Saxophonist, Band Leader, Advocate for Women in Music." Posted at www.peggygilbert.org/biography.html.

Reitz, Rosetta. Liner Notes, *The International Sweethearts of Rhythm.* 33rpm. Rosetta Records, 1984.

Simon, George T. *The Big Bands.* New York: Macmillan, 1967.

Treadwell, Bill. *Big Book of Swing.* New York: Cambridge House, 1946.

Tucker, Sherrie. *Swing Shift: "All-Girl" Bands of the 1940s.* Durham, NC: Duke University Press, 2000.

Walker, Leo. *The Big Band Almanac.* Revised ed. New York: Da Capo, 1989.

Ward, Geoffrey C., and Ken Burns. *Jazz: A History of America's Music.* New York: Knopf, 2002.

Washburn, Patrick S. *A Question of Sedition: The Federal Government's Investigation of the Black Press During World War II.* New York: Oxford University Press, 1986.

Periodicals

Various issues of *Band Leaders, Billboard, DownBeat, Liberty, Life,* and *Metronome* magazines (1940–1955) and the July 1942 issue of *All-American Band Leaders.*

Videos

Frances Carroll & "The Coquettes" (movie short featured on *Too Many Girls,* in three-disc set *The Lucy & Desi Movie Collection*). DVD. Warner Home Video, 2006.

Here Come the Co-eds. VHS. Universal, 2000. (It features the Hour of Charm.)

International Sweethearts of Rhythm: America's Hottest All-Girl Band. VHS. Jezebel Productions, 1986.

Jazz. Directed by Ken Burns, written by Geoffrey C. Ward. DVD. PBS Home Video, 2004.

Swing Era: Peggy Lee. DVD. Music Video Dist., 2004. (Features movie shorts of Ina Ray Hutton and Her Melodears, Lorraine Page and Her Orchestra, and Rita Rio and Her Mistresses of Rhythm.)

Recommended Reading

Bradley, James, with Ron Powers. *Flags of Our Fathers: Heroes of Iwo Jima.* New York: Delacorte, 2003.

Colman, Penny. *Rosie the Riveter: Women Working on the Home Front in World War II.* New York: Crown Books for Young Readers, 1998.

———. *Where the Action Was: Women War Correspondents in World War II.* New York: Crown Books for Young Readers, 2002.

Cooper, Michael L. *The Double V Campaign: African Americans and World War II.* New York: Dutton, 1998.

Harris, Jacqueline L. *The Tuskegee Airmen: Black Heroes of World War II.* Parsippany, NJ: Dillon, 1996.

Krull, Kathleen. *V Is for Victory: America Remembers World War II.* New York: Knopf Books for Young Readers, 2002.

Marsalis, Wynton. *Jazz ABZ.* New York: Candlewick, 2005.

Stanley, Jerry. *I Am an American: A True Story of Japanese Internment.* New York: Crown Books for Young Readers, 1994.

Recommended Listening

These are some of the CDs that kept me in the swing of things while working on this book.

Big Band Jazz: The Jubilee Sessions, 1943–1946. Hindsight Records, 1998.

Gal with a Horn. V.S.O.P. Records, 1995.

G.I. Jukebox: Songs from World War II. Hip-O Records, 1998.

Hot Licks: The International Sweethearts of Rhythm. Sounds of Yesteryear, 2006.

Ina Ray Hutton and Her Melodears. Vintage Music Productions, 2001.

Ina Ray Hutton and Her Orchestra. Soundcraft Records, 2000.

Songs That Got Us Through WWII, volumes I & II. Rhino Records, 1990, 1994.

Swing Time: Cocktail Hour. Columbia River Entertainment Group, 1999.

Valaida Snow: Queen of Trumpet & Song. DRG, 1999.

A Woman's Place Is in the Groove: Women in Jazz, 1923–1947. ABM, 2002.

The Women: Classic Female Jazz Artists, 1939–1952. RCA, 1991.

The Words and Music of World War II. Sony, 1991.

Illustration Credits

All visuals not credited below are from the author's collection.

Page 3: courtesy of Sony BMG Music Entertainment. Page 4: courtesy of the Library of Congress (#LC-USZ62-134893). Page 6, right: copyright © 1938 *Life* Inc. Reprinted with permission. All rights reserved. Page 7: courtesy of Vintage Music Productions. Page 9: courtesy of the Library of Congress (#LC-USZ62-125430). Page 10: courtesy of Culver Pictures (#1109-1103240). Page 11: copyright © 2006, VNU Businesss Media, Inc. Reproduced with permission from *Billboard*. Page 12: courtesy of Jane Sager. Page 13, top and bottom: courtesy of the Library of Congress (#LC-USW3-015859-D and #LC-USE6-D-009835). Page 19: courtesy of *DownBeat* magazine. Page 20: courtesy of Jane Sager. Page 23: courtesy of Photographs and Prints Division, Schomburg Center for Research in Black Culture, The New York Public Library, Astor, Lenox and Tilden Foundations (#SC-CN-88-0805: Anonymous. Portrait of Valaida Snow posing with baton, inscribed to "Sharp," ca. 1935). Page 26 and page 27, bottom: courtesy of Special Collections/Archives, John B. Coleman Library, Prairie View A&M University, Prairie View, Texas. Page 29: courtesy of the Estate of Eddie Durham. Page 30: courtesy of the United States Air Force. Page 31: courtesy of Special Collections/Archives, John B. Coleman Library, Prairie View A&M University, Prairie View, Texas. Page 32: Gjon Mili/Time & Life Pictures/Getty Images, courtesy of Getty Images. Page 33: courtesy of the Library of Congress (on master neg. #Np2388). Page 34: courtesy of Special Collections/Archives, John B. Coleman Library, Prairie View A&M University, Prairie View, Texas. Page 35: courtesy of Austin Hansen Collection, Photographs and Prints Division, Schomburg Center for Research in Black Culture, The New York Public Library, Astor, Lenox and Tilden Foundations (#SC-CN-96-0421: Austin Hansen. Exterior view of Apollo Theatre, 1940s. Photographs). Page 36: courtesy of Ernest Mae Crafton Miller. Page 42: courtesy of Louis Armstrong House and Archives. Page 45: courtesy of the Carnegie Museum of Art, Pittsburgh; Heinz Family Fund (acc. #2001.35.11001, Copyright © 2004 Carnegie Museum of Art, Charles "Teenie" Harris Archive). Page 47, top: courtesy of *DownBeat* magazine. Page 49: courtesy of Tony Fournier. Page 51, top, and page 52: courtesy of *DownBeat* magazine. Page 56: courtesy of the Peggy Gilbert Collection. Used with permission of the Ada Leonard Family. Page 58: courtesy of V.S.O.P. Records. Page 60: courtesy of Sherrie Tucker.

Text Credits

Excerpts from *DownBeat* articles on pp. 11, 14, 16, and 53 used by permission of *DownBeat* magazine. Excerpt from the *Nevada Journal* article on p. 52 used by permission of United Press International.

ACKNOWLEDGMENTS

Ever grateful to my editor, Erin Clarke, who kept the faith when, in the wake of several sorrows, my writing was more blues than jazz. Your understanding definitely helped get me into the swing of things. Big thanks, too, to others in the Random House crew for all your fabulous work and your cool: Artie Bennett, Melanie Chang, Sue Chodakiewicz, Kate Gartner, Nancy Hinkel, Alison Kolani, Jack Lienke, Carol Naughton, Carol Schneider, Adrienne Waintraub, and Allison Wortche.

Thank you *so much,* Sherrie Tucker, for being so blessedly free and easy with your knowledge and contact info.

Also in the gracious groove: Diana Carey (Radcliffe's Schlesinger Library); Marsha Durham (Executrix, Eddie Durham Estate); Tony Fournier (the Vocal Group Harmony Web Site, Vintage Group Harmony Show, and Yesterday USA SuperRadioStation); Deborah Gillaspie (Chicago Jazz Archive); David Haberstich (Archives Center of the National Museum of American History, Smithsonian Institution); Bill Hebden (Vintage Music Productions); Reuben Jackson (Duke Ellington Collection of the National Museum of American History, Smithsonian Institution); Peter Jacobson (V.S.O.P. Records); Chris Ogrodowski (Professional Musicians Local 47); and Jeannie Pool (filmmaker, *Peggy Gilbert & Her All-Girl Band*).

Thank you, Jane Sager, for the photos.

Thank you, Prairie View Co-Ed alumna Ernest Mae Crafton Miller, for the photo and the phone time.

Bless you, Phyllis Earles, University Archivist at Prairie View A&M, for going above and beyond when I was researching photos and facts.

Educator and all-genre scribe Kenny Carroll—you send me! Thanks for checking my jazz licks and letting me into your vast jazz brain. Another Kenny, hide-beater Kenneth Mills, was good enough to read a late draft of the manuscript. So were friend Bobby Thomas and his sister Nelta Gallemore, whose husband, Quintin (another hide-beater), was so good about my stream of questions.

And to my father, Willie Bolden: I know you hoped I would follow in your footsteps and take up the alto sax (or at least stick with clarinet), but you never missed a beat when you saw that with my art form, God had other plans. For that, I am eternally grateful.

Ada Leonard's All-American Girl
    Orchestra, 10–25, *12, 17,* 49, *56,*
    58, 61
    repertoire of, 15–16, 18
    salaries of, 13
    sexism toward, 13, 23–24
    USO shows by, 10–11, 13–14, 15
    wardrobe of, 13, 18, 19
American Federation of Musicians
    (AFM), 15, 25
Anna Jones's Western Swing Girls, 59
Apollo Theatre, 17, 22, 34–36, *35, 36,* 37,
    46, 48
Armstrong, Louie "Satchmo," 6, 41, 42,
    51
"At the Woodchoppers' Ball," 28

Babe Egan's Hollywood Redheads, 7
"Back Beat Boogie," 28, 34
Backstrom, Margaret "Padjo," 48
Basie, Count, 5, 6, 27, 28, 39, 51
Bennett, Will, 27, 28, *34*
Berigan, Bunny, 16, 21
Betty McGuire's Sub-Debs, 59
Big Book of Swing, 1, *51*
Bird, George "Red," 54
Blake, Eubie, 23, 35, 42
Blanche Calloway and Her Joy Boys, 5
Borde, Al, 11–12
Braddy, Pauline, *39,* 42, *43*
Bradley, Bettye, 31–33
Bryant, Clora, 26–27, 31, 34, *34, 58, 60*
"Bugle Call Rag," 13
Burnside, Viola "Vi," 46, 48, 52
Butler, Toby, 48, *49,* 53

Calloway, Cab, 5, *5,* 30
Carson, Norma, 18, 58
Carter, Consuela, 38
Cayler, Joy, *24*
"Chickery Chick," 25
Cole, Helen, 28, *34,* 36, 58
"Concerto for Trumpet," 14
Coquettes, 11, 15
Cortez, Alma, 38
Crafton, Ernest "Ernie" Mae, *34, 36,* 59
Cron, Rosalind "Roz," *49*

Darlings of Rhythm, *45,* 48, 53, 59
D'Artega, Al, 18
Daughters of Uncle Sam, 59
Davis, Bert Etta, *27, 34,* 58
Davis, Ernestine "Tiny," 46, 49, 58
de La Cruz, Nina, 38
Desmond, Johnny, 1, 51
Dixie Rhythm Girls, 59
Dixie Sweethearts, 59
Dixon, Lucille, *39, 43*
Dorsey, Tommy, 1, *6*
"Double V" campaign, 33

DownBeat, 5–6, 11, 14, 15, 16, 19, 46, 47,
    47, 48, *51,* 53
Durham, Eddie, *29,* 43, 47, 52

Eddie Durham's All-Star Girl Orchestra,
    29, 43
Eleanor Ten and Her Smoothies, 59
Ellington, Duke, 5, 6, *6,* 17, 27, 46, 51, 57

Fitzgerald, Ella, 1, *1,* 28, 30, 35
"Five Foot Two, Eyes of Blue," 57
Fourteen Bricktops, 59
Fred Harvey Company, 19–20, 22

Gale Agency, 29–31
Gilbert, Peggy, 20, *56*
Gillespie, Dizzy, 59
Glenn Miller Army Air Force Band, 51,
    55
Glenn Miller Band, 29, 51
Goodman, Benny, 1, *6,* 17
Graystone Ballroom, *6,* 40
Grigsby, Margaret, 31, 33, *34,* 57

Handy, D. Antoinette, 40
Handy, W. C., 1
Hardin, Lil, 42, *42*
Harlem Playgirls, 29, 48, 59
Hawkins, Erskine, 50
Henderson, Fletcher "Smack," 46–48
Herman, Woody, 14, 28
Holiday, Billie, 21, 35, 46
Hour of Charm, *3,* 12, 15, 58
Hutton, Ina Ray, *7,* 11, 13, 57, 60–61

"I Can't Get Started," 21
"I Don't Want to Set the World on Fire,"
    14, 29
"In the Mood," 5, 29
Ina Ray Hutton and Her Melodears, 7, *7,*
    29
International Sweethearts of Rhythm, 36,
    37–53, *39, 41, 43, 49, 50,* 57–58, 61
    finances of, 46, 52–53
    racial mix of, 38
    rift with Piney Woods School, 42–44
    transportation of, 40, *41*
    USO shows by, 50, 51–52
    wardrobe of, 45
"It Don't Mean a Thing (If It Ain't Got
    That Swing)," 5

James, Harry, 1, *1,* 4, 14, 28, 34, 46
jitterbug, *4,* 46
Joan Lee and Her Girl Orchestra, *19,* 59
Jones, Helen "T.D.," 38–40, *43,* 44
Jones, Laurence Clifton, 38, 39, 42
Jones, Rae Lee, 40, 44, 48
Jump Children, 37
"Jumpin' at the Woodside," 28, 29

King, Maurice, 52
Kirkpatrick, Ethel, 16
Krupa, Gene, 5, *5*, 15, 17–18

Lee, Joan, *19*, 59
Leonard, Ada, *10*, 11–13, *12*, 14, *56*, 57, 58
Liebman, Florence "Fagel," 16–18, 24–25, 58
Lindy Hop, 30, *32*
Lorraine Page and Her Orchestra, 59
Lucas, Roxanna, *39*, *43*, 46

Marian Pankey's Female Orchestra, 7
McGee, Evelyn, *41*, *43*
McGee, Nova Lee, 38
Miller, Glenn, 29, 51, 55

Office of War Information (OWI), 8, 9
"Once in a While," 14
"One O'Clock Jump," 5, 15, 29

Parker, Charlie, 59
Pearl Harbor, 7, 10, 13
Pettiford, Marjorie "Marge," *39*, *43*, 48
Pettiford, Oscar, 39, 59
Piney Woods Country Life School, 38, 40
    musical groups of, 38, 44
    rift with International Sweethearts of Rhythm, 42–44
Placksin, Sally, 7
Platinum Blondes of America, 59
Powell, Mel, *55*
Prairie View College, 26, *27*
    musical groups of, 28
Prairie View State College Co-Eds, 26–36, *26*, *31*, *34*, 37, 57, 58–59, 61
    formation of, 28
    transportation of, 31, 33, 34
    USO shows by, 30, 31, 33

Reitz, Rosetta, 48
Rice, Johnnie Mae, *39*, *43*
Rio, Rita, 11, *11*, 12
Rita Rio and Her Mistresses of Rhythm, 11, 12
Rogers, Sharon, *52*
Roosevelt, Franklin Delano, 22, 53

Sager, Janie, 10–11, 12, *12*, 13, 14, 16, 19–22, *20*, 56, 57, *60*
Saine, Helen, *39*, 40, *43*
Savoy Ballroom, 30, 46, 50
Sawyer, Mary, 14
Sepia Lassies of Harmony, 59
Sharon Rogers All-Girl Band, 52
Shaw, Artie, *6*, 29
Simon, George, 60–61
Slade, Brownie, 14
Smith, Viola, 14, *15*, 58
Snow, Valaida, 22, *23*

"Sophisticated Lady," 57
SPARS, 9, *51*
Spitalny, Phil, 3, 11, 15, 58
Starr, Jean, 47
'Stelle Slavin and Her Brunettes, 59
"Stompin' at the Savoy," 5
Stone, Jesse, 43, 52
"Sweethearts Jam," *48*
Swi-Bop, 58
swing
    definitions of, 1
    rise of, 3–5
    slang associated with, 4–5
"Swing Shift," 50
Swing Street, 22
Swinghearts, 3, 6, 7, 59
Swinging Rays of Rhythm, 44

Thomas, Elizabeth, 28, *34*
Thompson, Dez, *12*, 15
Treadwell, Bill, 1, 51
Truman, Harry S., 53
Tucker, Sherrie, 13, 15, 18, 21, 57, 60
Turner, Jessie, 53
Tuskegee Airmen, *30*, 33
"Tuxedo Junction," 50

USO (United Service Organizations), *13*
    camp shows sponsored by, 10–11, 13–14, *13*, 15, 24, 30, 31, 33, 50, 51–52

V-discs, 22–23, *25*
"Vi Vigor," 52
"Victory!" and "Double V" campaigns, 22–23, 33
Victory Belles, 20
Virgil Whyte's Musical Sweethearts, 31

WAACs (WACs), 9, 45
"White Cliffs of Dover," 14
Whyte, Trudy, 31
"Wild Party," 7
Williams, Cootie, 1, 28
Williams, Edna, 41, *43*
Wilson, Vi, 45
Winburn, Anna Mae, *43*, 46, 47, *47*, 52, 58
Wong, Willie Mae, *39*, *43*, 51–52
World War II
    casualties of, 21–22
    end of, 53
    internment camps during, 21
    rationing during, 18
    "Victory" movement during, 22–23, 33
    women in workforce during, 7–9, 28, 54–57
World's Fair, 10, 42

You Can't Ration Love, 18